MANUFACTURING
WITH
Heart
A HOLISTIC APPROACH

by

Loyal Peterman and Tanya Patrella

Manufacturing with Heart © 2015 Loyal Peterman and Tanya Patrella

For permission requests, please submit in writing to Manufacturing with Heart at the address below:

Manufacturing with Heart, Inc.
5475 Lake Shore Avenue
Westerville, OH 43082
www.manufacturingwithheart.com

Published by:
Smart Business Network
835 Sharon Dr., Suite 200
Westlake, OH 44145

Printed in the United States of America

Editor: Dustin S. Klein
Cover and Interior design: Randy Wood

ISBN: 978-0-9911081-7-6

Library of Congress Control Number: 2015937429

Acknowledgment

The authors would like to thank Christopher Richards, Lynnette Rogers, Dustin Klein, and Randy Wood for their help in bringing this book to life.

Editor's Note:

Loyal Peterman is best known to his friends and family as Butch. All references in the text to Butch are referring to the author, Loyal Peterman.

From our hearts to yours

Steve,

Hope this books gives you a perspective on how businesses can help change the world... in a good way.

All the Best to you as you journey to the restaurant of your dreams.

Just remember... it's the Journey itself that brings most joy!

Contents

Introduction

Twenty-first century American manufacturing is poised to reinvent itself—for the better. Old models and mindsets are giving way to a completely new paradigm: **Heart**.

Manufacturing with Heart explains how to transform your organization into a place of greater satisfaction for employees, customers, and stakeholders. You'll learn how to create a positive, profitable, and productive workplace where everybody wins.

Change starts at the top. As a manufacturing CEO or executive, reading this book is your first step. Instead of wasting time on silly distractions and conflicts, focus on what matters. If you want to move from surviving to thriving, this book is for you. The manufacturing landscape is rapidly changing. Behaviors that made you successful in the past are no longer relevant to a dynamic future. In this book you'll recognize the limits and challenges of 'business as usual.' But we are not offering Band-Aid solutions so your old structure can last just a little longer. Quick fixes usually ignore root causes. Rather, *Manufacturing with Heart* is a new way of thinking and behaving. It calls for global change in your organization. This is not for everyone.

It takes time and commitment. It takes courage for personal growth. Yet, if you can risk trusting people to be their best, if you have a strong desire for meaningful change, then this book will prepare you for a profitable and satisfying future.

All of us have a business culture, whether it's recognized or not. Culture is how we do things. It's how we treat each other. It's what we value. It's what we think of as normal codes of behavior. You'll learn why culture matters, and why examining basic beliefs can have profound impact on the way you do business. You'll see how you can influence and ultimately transform your manufacturing organization. You'll learn about our journey, and how we took a successful company and made it a better place to work, more profitable, and self-sustaining.

Leadership requires vision. But you knew that. What's just as important is courage, and the commitment to stay the course. Real change doesn't happen overnight. Manufacturing with Heart is not a pie-in-the-sky theory. We will roll up our sleeves, pull back the curtain, and show you how we did it. You'll hear what employees say about their experience. We show how we created a place of inclusiveness, collaboration, and trust; a place where improved communication leads to better and faster decision making; a place where it became a lot more fun to run—and work for—a manufacturing company.

At first, some of our concepts may seem strange. But we will explain what we mean, and do so in straightforward English—without technical jargon. We've included a glossary of words and ideas that may be unfamiliar. Our goal is to make complexity as simple as possible. Or, as Albert Einstein said, "Things should be as simple as possible, but no simpler." You'll see why paying attention to the words we use matters. Words are powerful, and word choice can cause apathy and disconnection, or inclusion, respect, and motivation—it's really up to you. Each chapter ends with a "heartbeat" that summarizes the main points for rapid access.

Manufacturing with Heart is a holistic method. In other words, it addresses everything—how the big picture and the details are interconnected. Small changes can have large effects. Manufacturing with Heart connects everyone in the organization in new ways. You'll understand the underpinnings of heart culture, why they matter, and how they show up as behavior in a manufacturing organization.

Our new model brings together two elements: *Heart culture* and a *process-centered organization* (PCO). PCO replaces single-task focus with a holistic process—an integrated collection of tasks. New ways of doing things lead to new insights, and new insights lead to more satisfying, productive, and meaningful behavior. Each iteration pumps new life into your ever-evolving organization, so the organization actually learns from itself. As a CEO, this means that you have more time to steer your organization toward a better future.

Today, the next generation is entering the world of work. Manufacturers who want to remain relevant must attract engaged young employees. You'll discover what Millennials are looking for as they come into the manufacturing workplace—and it's not just a paycheck.

We wrote this book to share our knowledge and excitement about what's possible. We did it and so can you.

Welcome! Come along with us. We hope you enjoy the ride.

Part One

A Holistic Approach

Chapter One

Our World

What's Possible?

Is it possible to create a work culture that produces profitability and self-sustaining value for everyone in your organization? How great would it be if people anticipated coming to work each day because they wanted to contribute their best to the group effort?

Imagine a place where agile systems quickly adapt to new demands; where your technology boosts production; and everyone has access to the information, equipment, and processes they need.

Is it possible a manufacturing company's structure could generate a place where conflict has given way to productivity-boosting cooperation? Can you imagine spreading happiness at work?

This is not a fantasy. We did it.

Change starts with an idea, an imagined possibility. Take a minute. Think what it would be like for you if your organization abandoned supervision, and replaced it with help and advice. Imagine if people on the factory floor understood the whole manufacturing process and had the ability to work together unsupervised. Imagine how they would fix problems and keep the whole process running smoothly as part of a complete adaptive system. Can you picture it? If you can't, you're not unusual. But we know it's possible.

Like you, most CEOs of manufacturing companies want to redirect time, attention, and effort to those things that matter most. Why not spend your time leading your company to new frontiers instead of fixing problems?

Think about a plant where people learn to develop themselves so they become more responsive and responsible. Consider what it would be like if your company was a place of growth for everyone. What if people in your organization were able to talk to each other in a way that reflected mutual respect and common purpose? Could manufacturing life be fun, easier, and more satisfying? Absolutely!

We Make Stuff

That's what manufacturers do—we make stuff. Manufacturing in the United States is being reborn. There are exciting developments in our industry. We manufacturers have learned a few collective lessons. We've discovered the limits of off-shoring. Events elsewhere have an impact at home. Chinese workers are no longer content with low wages as standards of living rise. Consequently, off-shoring is not so profitable for U.S. companies. As American manufacturing is reestablishing itself, now is the perfect time to look at new realities. Jobs that are coming back are not the old jobs. Technologies like 3-D printing, robotics, and CNC are changing the face of manufacturing. But first, let's take a step back in order to leap forward.

16

The period directly after World War II was a great time to be a U.S. manufacturer. European and Asian industrial competitors had been flattened by war while U.S. factories remained unharmed and were prospering. Demand for durable goods fueled growth. Wages and productivity increased. Our economy took off. According to a report by the Bureau of Labor Statistics, manufacturing employment grew steadily in the 1950s until it reached its peak in 1979.

Time and motion studies, introduced in the late 1800s by Frederick Taylor, as well as Frank and Lillian Gilbreth, originally looked at workers as machines. Every action was measured in the quest for greater efficiencies. Up until about 1920, this was the era of organization as machine. Task efficiency reigned supreme. The mindset was don't ask questions. Get on with your work.

Command and control management pulled us through the Industrial Revolution. It persists. Even today, some still view peoplepower as machines with flexibility. But this is changing as businesses realize the future must be different. How to accomplish this difference is our story.

From 1920 to 1940, the next organizational evolution started to emerge. Instead of organization as machine, the new metaphor was organization as organism, a living thing. General systems theory came from the science of evolutionary biology. Organizations had systems within systems, just as the human body has nervous, circulatory, and digestive systems. Yet dissecting a human body won't let you locate intelligence or ideas. The whole organism is greater than the sum of its parts. Both machine and organism metaphors came from a purely scientific perspective: physics and biology.

Since our species came into existence we have survived by working together. We're hard-wired to be tribal. We act in meaningful ways that can't be explained by science. Emotional drives, a sense of belonging, customs, individual development, satisfactions—and even fun—had been previously ignored in our industry. Appreciation of culture pays dividends, as you can see from any "Best Places to Work" list. Employers have talked and written about how their employees are their most valuable asset. But until now talk and action have been at odds with each other. We'll go into reasons and remedies later.

We humans are social. We have ceremonies and rituals that tell us who we are as a group. Culture creates meaning, and embodies organizational self-knowledge. In the best way it acts as a constraint on the whims of individual leaders. Culture's power is that it binds people together in a common purpose.

To reduce costs, companies previously trained only one person on a task or piece of equipment. Consequently, manufacturers were vulnerable to the limits of worker overspecialization. Know-how was guarded, and restricted to a narrow boundary of technique. Parts could only be made by specialists who had no incentive to share their skill. But rapid change in technology means we can no longer rely on hiring people with specific skills and then expect their skills to last.

Today's workers need higher levels of technical competence. But even that's not enough. Smart employers look for employees with potential to learn quickly; people who are flexible and cooperative. Sustained profitability requires effective and inclusive collaboration.

AT's Humble Roots—Butch's Story

The Abrasive Technology (AT) story begins in the winter of 1970 with me, Loyal M. (Butch) Peterman, Jr. , and three other young men. We were working for General Electric Superabrasives and began talking about what it would be like to run our own company. We wanted to build a reputable business that made high-quality diamond tools. We also wanted to think long-term, keep things as simple as possible, and pay our bills on time with cash.

Talk soon turned to action. With less than $20,000 in capital, the safety of paychecks was left behind. We had no experience running a business, and no manufacturing plant. We didn't have financing, products, or even customers. What we did have was drive, belief, and desire.

Together as partners, we worked day and night, including weekends, developing, testing, and making product, and designing a new brochure. We talked a lot about business values and methodology. The focus was on how we were to make it through the next day, the next week, and the next month. Long-term planning was yet to come.

Early successes were encouraging. Passion and perseverance drove our group on during the 1970s and 1980s. We set high standards. AT was ahead of competitors with computer technology and newly simplified manufacturing processes. Desire to be the best became the natural way of being.

But it wasn't all sunshine and roses. AT's credibility for customer service was severely tested early on. We sold a large tool order to a Dayton, Ohio company, the largest order of industrial products thus far. Unfortunately, the customer wasn't happy with the product and wanted to return all of it. Since AT's credo was customer satisfaction, we took back the tools for credit. Even though it hurt AT financially, other customers took notice of the company's commitment to its product, and business expanded.

Focus now was on niche capabilities of high-quality, superabrasive products. AT expanded internal capacity. New agile systems delivered specialty needs fast.

AT decided what it didn't want to make. The company looked to the future with a view to sustainability of long-term growth markets. If AT was to continue to grow, it needed to broaden its markets and geography. This has been borne out over the years—when one market is down, another is up. In the early stages, AT's intention was to grow organically at no more than 20 percent a year. Anything more would stress organization, systems, and people beyond their capabilities.

Over time, AT continued to find new markets, expanding products into dentistry, watchmaking, stained glass, optical, automotive, and aerospace industries. We even made tools that crafted the heat-shield of the space shuttle.

Just like every manufacturer at the time, AT modeled what other companies were doing. As capability grew, the company added people to make and sell industrial products. AT began to develop a hierarchical structure, adding vice presidents, managers, supervisors, and coordinators. But organizational change at the company was soon to come.

Well-known management guru Peter Drucker's ideas about business culture raised questions and ignited discussion among managers in the 1970s and '80s. Drucker remains the best known management guru of his time. For him, management was a 20th

Century social innovation responsible for increasing quality of life, technological progress, and even avoidance of global conflict. Drucker promoted his vision of corporation as a society where decentralized decision making became normal behavior.

In the 1990s, radical change ideas were filtering through the business world. Engineer and business writer Michael Hammer's ideas shifted AT's focus to an organizational structure where rapid decision making would become the norm. At the time, there was a lot of writing and discussion of Hammer's work. Many academics agreed this was the way it ought to be. The problem was nobody actually knew how to do it.

These were great ideas in and of themselves. Many companies tried to implement change in either culture or organizational structure—but not both together. Most efforts failed.

By 1992, three AT partners were gone, leaving me as sole owner and CEO. AT was now perfectly positioned to take advantage of new ideas and to discover how to put them into practice. It was a solid, profitable company. We made excellent products and still do. We had good customers and great, experienced employees. And, with all this in mind, I looked deep within myself and asked, "What do I want to do with all this?"

I realized I wanted to focus my energies on building an organization where everyone gets to contribute, everyone gets to gain, and everyone learns and grows. I wanted to create an environment where each person enjoys working every day. There are statistics that say 80 percent of American workers hate their jobs. I wanted a company where at least 80 percent love their jobs. And I'm very proud to say that we have come a long way toward that goal. But a lot had to change to achieve a bright future for the business.

AT Gets A Heart Transplant—Enter Tanya Patrella

In 1994, things changed. Tanya Patrella, then a member of AT's leadership team, and I began a relationship with the Center for Creative Leadership (CCL), a global, non-profit specializing in leadership development, teambuilding, and change management. Tanya had become a valuable member of the team, and soon would become integral in transforming the business. This is where our stories intertwined—setting us on a path that eventually became *Manufacturing with Heart*.

When we first met with CCL to see what they could offer us, we weren't convinced by their presentation. We weren't sure they were forward thinking enough for the changes we wanted.

As we were ready to leave, their executive vice president picked up on our disappointment. He said we should meet Gary Rhodes at CCL. Gary was responsible for strange or unusual questions or projects. Now, 20 years later, we continue to have a great, ongoing relationship with Gary and other CCL fellows. Even though Gary's been retired from CCL he still advises us.

The company was a tremendous resource. Our initial project, leadership training for managers, soon expanded to include all associates. At first, this involved significant analysis of personality and communication types, based on the belief that self-understanding is the foundation of individual development. Change—and embracing it—soon became an ongoing initiative. Through 2000, managers at AT worked tirelessly to grow the business while guiding employees through continual change. The CEO's job was redefined as "lead by creating a culture of trust." Some of the early tools introduced were:

- State-of-the art technologies
- Monetary incentives for team work

- Employee education, including a reading and study program for product flow
- Language changes, such as "employees" to "associates" and "manage" to "lead"
- Leadership development
- Personal development for everyone
- Continuous two-way communications about the business

With this groundwork to create a culture of trust, in 2001 the leadership team implemented a radical new *process-centered organization* (PCO). From its inception, PCO has been a flexible work in progress. It built upon Hammer's re-engineering concept, an idea first proposed in 1990 in *Harvard Business Review*. PCO is a fundamental analysis and redesign of how things get done and who gets to do them. Implemented redesign created tighter bonds among everyone in the company. And it was trial by ordeal that ultimately proved successful. AT lost orders, closed plants, and laid off 20 percent of its workforce during the global downturn of 2007–2009. These difficulties tested the new structure. But trust built up over the previous decade saved the day, and AT remained resilient.

Shared Learning—A New Beginning

In 2013, we (Butch and Tanya) formed a new company called Manufacturing with Heart (MwH) to share what we've learned with others. Since January 1, 2014, Daryl Peterman, Butch's son, has run AT's global businesses. He leads a solid, profitable company, with good products, good customers, and great, experienced employees who have become involved associates demonstrating strong leadership.

MwH's core belief comes from our experience with AT: Most people want to do good work, give of their best, be trusted, and have a chance to grow. Every company AT purchased became a happier and more productive place to work. And we had a lot of fun making that happen.

We're excited to share what we've learned. This book is about personal, organizational, and process development, and how they are bound together in what we describe as holistic manufacturing.

There will always be resistance to anything new. Long ago, nasty things happened to people who suggested the crazy idea that the world was round. There always has been, and always will be, objections to that which is different. Orthodoxy shuts out innovation. So this book is not for everyone. If your purpose is to simply squeeze more short-term profit from your organization, then you're not going to like what we have to say. Manufacturing with Heart requires time, persistence, and patience.

Smaller manufacturing organizations have an advantage. A combination of size, organization, entrenched systems, and culture constrain most large organizations, so they reject wholesale change. There are exceptions, of course, but ill-considered incentives can work against sustainable and reputable evolutionary growth. For example, reward for inappropriate sales orders can be unprofitable for the company. One consequence is that it can pit sales and production against each other. Organization and culture are constantly in tension. Shareholders demand instant gratification at the expense of long-term perspectives. Talk about creativity is accepted, but complex bureaucracies resist radically different behavior. Happily, this is not the case for smaller manufacturers. Real change happens at the edges, and it starts with you. Change, as you might expect, requires courage. Stay with us if you want more long-term profitability, satisfaction, and sustainability—the best, as they say, it yet to come.

Beyond Carrots and Sticks

Trust is the foundation of successful cooperative effort. AT succeeded in building an environment where everyone likes coming to work. There have been a few surprises along the way. We found that given more autonomy, people are far more productive. For example, instead of setting production quotas, we just asked people to make as much as they could. Productivity skyrocketed. Why? It was the heart culture.

A culture of fear has predominated manufacturing since the Industrial Revolution. Untapped creative potential was left to wither. Most people want to use their best selves at work, but that can only happen if culture supports and encourages some level of autonomy. Your company's culture is in your and your employees' hands.

People usually behave as they're treated. A culture of fear requires constant surveillance. Supervisors manage. Those who have power "empower" the powerless. This is not a culture to foster capability, respect, and dignity. The assumption is people will not work unless made to, and then they'll do as little as possible. Sweatshops aren't known for their innovation. A culture of fear hides information. It motivates by using sticks and carrots. But what if neither stick nor carrot were necessary? We've found an elegant third way.

Can you really think of yourself as successful if your work leaves you stressed and unhappy even when your cash flow is at high tide? We don't believe so. Our mission at Manufacturing with Heart is to help others cultivate a positive and productive workplace. We are realists. We acknowledge that profitability is the life blood of any organization. Yet culture has a direct and positive relationship with the bottom line. Many of its benefits, as you will see, go beyond dollars and cents.

Look around you. Change in our manufacturing world is accelerating. We've shifted from a repetitive, skill-based, task focus to rapid adoption of new processes. Baby boomers are retiring and their experience and expertise is walking out the door with them. Enter Generation Y, the Millennials.

These generations, born between 1980 and 2000, are different. They want a work culture that encourages self-development, professional learning, and autonomy. Millennials tend to volunteer more. They live and breathe technology. No cohort has been so interconnected. They've grown up constantly linked to their peers. Smartphones are almost part of their bodies. They expect technology to be easy to use and in place to do their jobs. Constant improvement is the norm.

Millennials know how to collaborate. They've embraced the sharing economy. Zipcar, Airbnb, and Uber put idle resources to use through sharing. Economic forces are responsible for this shift in values. According to research by the Joint Center for Housing Studies at Harvard University, home ownership fell by 12 percent between 2006 and 2011 for those under age 35.[1] Automobile ownership is down for this group, too. Attitudes are changing. Shared housing is common. But everyone's smartphone is a necessity. Connection and collaboration are what Millennials do. Accordingly, manufacturing needs a new model.

---

1   http://www.theatlantic.com/magazine/archive/2012/09/the-cheapest-generation/309060/2/

Holistic Manufacturing

In medicine, a holistic approach treats the whole person, not just symptoms. Holistic manufacturing takes into account interconnections of all parts of the business. The concept of stakeholder extends to everyone impacted by the activities of your company. Change one thing, affect everything. There are four key components of holistic manufacturing: core beliefs, technology, organization and culture. They manifest best as part of heart culture.

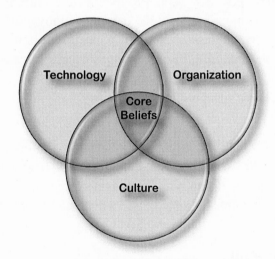

Figure 1: Core Beliefs permeate a holistic organization

Core beliefs permeate every aspect of the holistic approach. Whether or not they are widely recognized, all manufacturers' business models operate from core beliefs. Those beliefs can lead a company to bright futures or sink into *stuckiness*—paralyzing fear and blame. Beliefs are so important that we've devoted the next chapter to discussing them.

Technology is all of the tools and know-how required to develop, manufacture, and market products—including equipment, processes, and information systems. Be early adopters of concepts and technologies, simplify them, and create methodologies that can actually be implemented.

Organization is a structure for product, process, and information flow. We'll have more to say about developing a process-centered organization in chapters three and four. A responsive organization makes faster decisions and can rapidly allocate and deploy necessary resources.

Culture governs behavior. Neglected culture smothers possibility. Done right, culture enlivens innovation. Attitudes and behaviors change over time. Culture continually defines what we pay attention to as a group—and what we ignore. A focus only on task metrics has caused many of us to ignore its importance as a resource for profitability.

Heart culture is an evolutionary advance in collective productivity. It is the lifeblood of a people-oriented learning business. Belief in people, trust, capability, and feeling is primary. Holistic Manufacturing with Heart seeks to balance the needs of everyone: customers, employees, owners, and suppliers.

Attitudes Evolve

There's a saying that if fish could think, they'd be the last to discover water. Attitudes we experience every day seem normal to us so we don't look at what might be better. Opportunities can stare us in the face without us recognizing them. The psychological term for this is *inattentional blindness*. We can fool ourselves into seeing only what we want to see.

It's difficult to grasp attitudes of the past. During the 18th century, tourists liked to view the unfortunate inmates of "insane asylums" and even paid for the privilege of poking them with a long pole.[2] Horrific procedures were fostered on asylum inmates as recently as 1960.

In the 1960s, TV commercials promoted doctor-recommended cigarettes. Today, the medical establishment has wised up. Back then, women in the airline business (to name just one industry) were forced to leave their jobs when they married. These attitudes seemed normal at the time, but change in outlook is a fact of life.

Technology has come a long way in manufacturing, but so too has mindset. The Industrial Revolution was an earlier stage in human and economic development. Children labored alongside adults for long hours, often sleeping on the factory floor. Many never made it to adulthood. Beer was the only available drink because water was polluted. You can imagine what a combination of alcohol and dangerous machinery did. Many factory workers were maimed and died because of dangerous working conditions. Disease was rife. Factory workers lived in squalid conditions. They were seen as expendable. Lives were miserable and short.

Attitudes have become progressively better over time. Yet skill-based hiring is a legacy from the 19th century. The mechanical mindset persists, for example, in the curiosity-killing "teaching to the test" in school. We can become so enthusiastic about success that we misapply the same solution to every problem. Mechanical efficiency was such a successful driver of prosperity that all other values were quashed. We're not arguing against efficiency. Rather, we need efficient systems and effective behaviors. But a focus on efficiency alone blinds us to opportunities because we're looking in the wrong direction. As the saying goes, "To a hammer, everything looks like a nail."

---

2   http://www.asylum.com/2010/02/02/famous-notorious-abandoned-haunted-insane-asylums/

Conformity

Should people fit manufacturing systems, or should manufacturing processes fit people? The Procrustean bed is a metaphor for rigidity. The Greek myth of Procrustes illustrates a point about inflexibility and the price of efficiency. Procrustes was a scoundrel, reputed to be son of the god Poseidon. He lived beside the road between Athens and Eleusis. Seeming to be a generous host, he invited travelers to spend the night. He had two beds, one short and one long. Procrustes tied his victims to a long bed if they were short and a short bed if they were long. He made them fit his bed by stretching them or chopping off limbs. His story concludes when Procrustes gets a dose of his own medicine.

Too much conformity and too many rules limit what can be done. This doesn't mean you can throw away the rules and expect things to be better. They won't be. The ground needs preparing first, as we will explain. Technology strives to be ever more intuitive. This is true for every aspect of manufacturing. The old way of making everyone conform to overly rigid structures is dehumanizing. What people might bring of themselves to the workplace is restricted. Human beings don't work like machines. Human value is not just material. It's potential: access to ideas, health, openings for self-development, and collective creativity.

Developing

Business people usually think of growth as expansion of capital, markets, resources, and profit. But evolution's multi-directional growth includes workers' self-development. This is holistic manufacturing, which can be better understood by introducing the concept of the *holon*.

A holon is a basic unit, and complete system in itself. At the same time, every holon is part of a larger system. For example, atoms are things in themselves. Molecules are a collection of atoms. A molecule has a distinct identity, yet it's also a thing in itself and it includes atoms. Molecules combine to form more complex structures, and so on.

The mantra here is "transcend and include." Holonic development operates in stages. Each new stage includes previous stages and transcends them. Each stage in child development produces more complexity, and includes all previous stages. Communication starts with a baby's turning toward a stimulus. Baby smiles at mom. Later, the child makes gestures and vocalizations. Later still, language evolves. Each stage transcends the stage before it. At each phase, the learner has a greater number of behaviors available than previously. Development leads to more possibilities and a bigger repertoire of responses.

A single person is a holon. A group of people is a more complex holon, made up of numerous individuals.

The capabilities of a work group transcend the capabilities of any one individual in the team. All the teams together make up the holonic body of the corporation.

As each individual in a team becomes better skilled, expands capabilities, and improves inter-personal communication, the more capable becomes the workgroup. You move from rules to guidelines to suggestions. As each person is more functional, the whole team benefits. As each team is more effective, so is your company. You're able to focus on what matters.

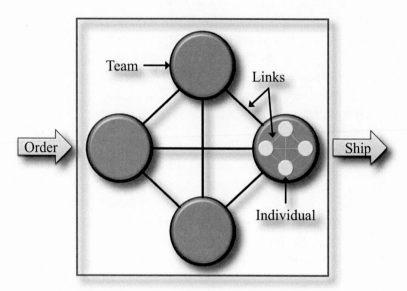

Figure 2: A linked, manufacturing holonic organization

Potential

Positive regard for individuals is a central idea of *Manufacturing with Heart*. Abraham Maslow's work on human behavior and motivation has influenced generations of management practitioners. Drucker was one of them. We believe Maslow was right when he claimed that our capabilities clamor to be used.

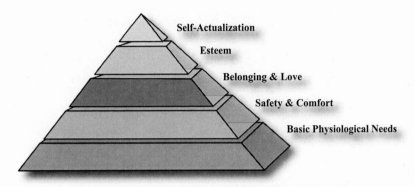

Figure 3: Abraham Maslow's Hierarchy of Needs

Maslow's idea of self-actualization came at the top of his hierarchy of needs. His model is usually represented as a triangle. Survival needs form the base. Air, water, sleep, and other such essentials have to be met in order for us to stay alive. Only once these are fulfilled can we pay attention to "higher" needs. Safety and security make up the next level. You can't think of safety and security if you're about to die of thirst. All you think of is water. Once security needs are met, we can progress to social needs of family and friendship. The desire for confidence-building achievement comes next. While we're in lower levels of development, we need more structure to function. This is why we need rules. Higher developmental levels allow for flexibility and greater understanding of the whole system.

At the apex of the triangle is self-actualization. Self-actualization is authentic motivation: the courage to try things out, develop our own ideas, learn from mistakes, and make decisions. Self-actualization means to act with autonomy and responsibility. Each of us has potential. We either develop it or we don't. Culture either encourages self-actualization or limits it. But self-actualization can't happen unless earlier stages of development are met.

Maslow believed that enlightened management was impossible in an authoritarian society. Command and control limits self-expression. This is why authoritarian organizations can talk about creativity but can't implement it. Minds and hearts have to change first.

Synergy (an expression Maslow coined) encompasses the individual and the group. Everyone wins when personal and organizational goals align. Friction diminishes. What's good for one person is good for the group.

Trying to impose a new structure without understanding how it operates always results in failure. We need preparation for collective change. And this is why changing your company starts with your own self-development.

Reaching Out

We knew we needed some help. Leadership concepts seemed like the right place to start. We wanted to be leaders who remove obstacles and provide information and resources for people to do their jobs. We wanted to create a self-perpetuating culture where everyone wins.

So we invested heavily in personal development. CCL helped us learn more about ourselves and what leadership means. Most of us resisted the necessity of slow change. We naturally wanted everything to happen quickly, but we came to the realization that cultural change evolves over time. Time allows for acceptance and absorption, but the moment has to be right. Even when it is, expect resistance. Looking at beliefs is the first step, and that's the topic of our next chapter.

Heartbeat

- Our manufacturing world is changing fast.
- Holistic manufacturing rests on four elements: core beliefs, organization, technology, and culture.
- People want to develop themselves, but this can happen only if the four elements are in place to support them.
- The combination of a Trust Culture + PCO leads to Manufacturing with Heart.
- Small manufacturing organizations have the advantage.
- Policy needs to match intentions.
- Positive culture change is possible: expect resistance.
- Millennials need a different kind of workplace.
- New possibilities start with you.

Chapter Two

Beliefs: The Basis
of Heart Culture

B*elief drives everything.* Beliefs are fundamental to the way we see the world. They engage our instinctual and emotional selves. Guiding principles emerge from what we believe. Beliefs shape perspective, which is why they're worth looking at.

Belief speaks to the heart. If you want commitment and aligned action, then your company's principles need to embody sincere personal beliefs of stakeholders. Defining your own beliefs allows you to critically evaluate your existing principles. This is the first step toward greater understanding of yourself, of those around you, and of your organizational norms.

Belief has immense power for good or ill. Psychosomatic illness is a reality. You can worry yourself sick imagining events that might never happen. But imagine the opposite—psychosomatic health. A placebo pill can make you better because you believe it will. Now extend that idea to your whole organization. Can you believe in creating a manufacturing environment that's successful, efficient, productive, and a place people want to come to work; a place of dignity, learning, respect, and fun? First you have to imagine it.

Belief focuses attention. You've heard the expression, "seeing is believing." But believing is a way of seeing. Believing determines behavior. Existing belief filters what you see and what you ignore. It either limits or expands possibilities. If you look hard enough, you'll usually find what you're looking for.

If you look for mistakes, you'll find them. If you look for people giving of their best, you're likely to find that, too. If you believe it's a dog-eat-dog world, then you'll spend a lot of time baring your teeth. Conflict and hostility do exist, but so do their opposite. If you look for people smiling, then that's what you're likely to see.

Belief is interpretation. How you treat other people isn't based on how they are, but on your opinion of them. We interpret our experience based on our beliefs. Shakespeare's character Hamlet spoke of this timeless wisdom when he said, "[F]or there is nothing either good or bad, but thinking makes it so." You see people who are underperforming. It's easy to jump to the conclusion they're lazy. But what looks like laziness could be exhaustion. Just maybe the person you think of as lazy was up all night with a newborn or had a medical emergency. Everyone can identify physical exhaustion, but there is mental exhaustion, too. Being overwhelmed saps energy. You could judge a person to be confused when really they're just unfamiliar with a situation. We all learn at different speeds.

Belief is personal. This doesn't mean exclusive. We have beliefs in common. This is what bonds groups together as community. But belief is a personal experience that creates meaning for an individual, and like snowflakes each of us is unique. Personal feeling is important to us. Throughout history untold numbers of people have died for their beliefs. ***Belief tells us who we are.***

Belief (sometimes) trumps logic. Because belief operates in the domain of feeling, in times of blind enthusiasm such as during stock-market bubbles, or under threat or stress, belief can override the thinking parts of our brain. When this happens, instinct takes over. Extreme conditions get in the way of thinking.

Belief is infectious. Enthusiasm is catching, but so is despair. And this is why creating a workplace where people are given the chance to demonstrate more of who they are and what they can do makes sense.

Belief matters. We can measure results, such as turnover rates, innovation, or people smiling at work. But it's time to take a second look at the old saying, "What gets measured gets done." Our industry's default view is to look for measurable results. There is nothing wrong with this. It's the scientific way.

Feelings are difficult to measure in a meaningful way. Emotional life is fundamental to the human experience and can't be reduced to a pie chart. If we claim we are 20 percent sad, 30 percent mad, and 50 percent happy, it doesn't tell us much. We don't experience our emotional selves this way. Human emotion is far more complex and nuanced. Science is a powerful and effective discipline. We must have a scientific outlook, but too often think science is the only game in town. It's not.

Sigmund Freud gave up working with hypnotism, not because it didn't work (it did), but because it couldn't be measured. Hypnotism couldn't be systematically reproduced and therefore wasn't considered scientific. At the time, the new discipline of psychoanalysis was desperate to claim the legitimacy science would bestow. The danger here for us is we ignore what we can't measure. That's a mistake.

Science doesn't have a lot to say about belief. Science can't grasp human experience such as love, loyalty, gratitude, or meaning. It can measure what people say about these things, but not much about the feeling experience itself. Belief isn't something you can examine on the laboratory bench. But belief, like storytelling, has immense power.

Beliefs Change

In the 1930s, management beliefs were changing in what became known as the Human Relations Movement. Instead of worker-as-machine, employee psychology became the object of study. Douglas McGregor's book, *The Human Side of Enterprise* (1960), made distinctions between Theory X and Theory Y.

Command and control Theory X treats workers as disconnected, incapable of anything but the most fundamental tasks. The predominant managerial belief of Theory X is that workers are disengaged. Theory X management bases its actions on the core belief that workers need watching because they're lazy and will do as little as possible. This was the view of Frederick W. Taylor. His Pennsylvania tombstone reads: The father of scientific management.

Taylor believed machines would replace man. Industry took up his ideas with enthusiasm. Time and motion studies were designed to make humans as efficient as machines. *Taylorism*, as it became known, happened at a time of great economic change. Unskilled farm workers were moving to cities to work in industry. Taylor's contribution was to rapidly turn these farmers into skilled workers. He instituted organizational efficiencies to create a workplace where thinking wasn't required. There was no place for humanistic beliefs in industry at the time.

Theory Y's core belief is different. Employees enjoy self-directed work in pursuit of corporate goals. Motivation is an inherent quality. Management's job, according to this belief, is to maintain employee commitment in an environment of trust, learning, open communication, and minimal supervision.

Theory X operates by surveillance, Theory Y by support.

Today, merely stating guiding principles with no regard for the current reality or for examining beliefs is only too common. This is the problem with theories in general.

Why Theories Fail

Imposing a theory without understanding the existing structure is an act of violence. It's like an enemy occupation and encourages resistance— much to the surprise of many who've tried it. Turning theory into practice can only happen when beliefs that inform principles are genuine.

Real motivation for change comes with preparation. The idea is to form an alliance of heart and mind. This requires time-consuming, face-to-face interaction with each individual in the organization. In larger companies hurdles are higher—often much higher.

Theories can't simply be put into practice piecemeal. They have to be aligned holistically with organizational structure, culture, and relevant technology. Early attempts at implementing Theory Y failed due to autonomy without adequate organizational structure and cultural support. Maslow was an early enthusiast of Theory Y, but over time he came to see problems with it.

Experience with Theory Y showed that not everyone was capable of higher level behavior. Maslow thought that the theory didn't serve those not suited to complex functioning.

Despite Theory Y's failure, it's not without merit. It was an early evolution. The danger was throwing the baby out with the bath water. As the limiting belief goes, if Theory Y doesn't work, then revert to Theory X. Instead of stepping backward in that way, we could instead move further forward, or to the side. There are more options if only we choose to look for them. Do your beliefs limit or expand options?

Expect (Some) Resistance

There are always people who resist change. There are people who want to disrupt anything new. There is no place in a healthy workplace for passive-aggression. But passive-aggression may be a result of a repressive culture where people have no way to express legitimate concerns. Nevertheless, no employer can afford subversion, just as no civilized society can be safe with violent criminals on the streets. Something must be done. In the case of chronic disruptive behavior, that may be eventual dismissal

When it comes to people who think they're a one-task-only specialist, you can improve the situation. Before you make quick judgments, consider introducing small steps. Perhaps the individual can learn just one more task. A next or previous task along the line is a good start. Such an incremental achievement may be resisted at first, but even small success builds confidence. Boundaries can expand.

Boundary Belief

A boundary is a limit, a container, or an operational territory. It protects. What it protects could be a belief, a process, a habit, an assumption, or a perspective. Some people work better within firm boundaries; others work well with more porous boundaries. The challenge is to find the balance. Even the most self-directed person needs some limits. There are four types of boundaries, as described by Joseph Luft and Harry Ingham in their Johari window:

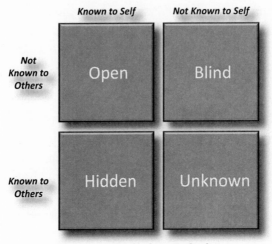

Figure 4: Boundary Belief

1. Everyone knows about it
2. You know about it, but other people don't
3. Other people know about it but you don't
4. You run into it by accident.

Discussion of boundaries is important because normally if people violate a boundary they get yelled at. But it doesn't have to be that way.

Taboo is anything outside of an accepted code of behavior. Talking about boundaries creates an opening to challenge existing beliefs. Some managers are afraid of what they might discover. As organizational consultant Warren G. Bennis put it, "Managers do things right; leaders do the right thing." Doing things right for managers has traditionally meant policing boundaries—not examining them. Yet even the person who's making the boundary may not have known it was there until someone stumbled into it.

Examining a boundary is a chance for valuable conversations, especially around the concept of being allowed to make mistakes. Bennis wrote that early success is a problem for companies because they don't get a chance to learn from their errors.

We interpret the experience of crossing a boundary. We remember what happened and draw conclusions. We do this at an early age. It's how we learn. Sometimes our conclusions are straightforward. The infant touches the hot stove once, but not again (usually). But for adults, most experience in the workplace is not so straightforward. We interpret what goes on, but experience is the teacher.

Questioning Boundaries

What one person believes is a mistake, another person can see as opportunity to learn. Once you have flexibility to look at beliefs about boundaries, the conversation becomes more open, interesting, and practical. Flexibility to discuss restrictions without a lot of negativity comes from your willingness to be vulnerable and open to change the boundary. This allows a real possibility of evolutionary growth. Boundaries can be changed. You can ask questions:

- Should the boundary be there?
- What is its function?
- How does it serve the individual and the organization?
- How flexible should this boundary be?
- Should it be a rule or a guideline?

- Was the boundary arbitrary?
- Does it still make sense?
- Is now the time for change?
- Do we need to expand or reduce it?

Touch Time, Food, and Stories—Butch's Perspective

When I became general manager of AT, I started having lunch with everyone in the company. In a culture of management by fear this just doesn't happen: hierarchy and disrespect prevent genuine connection. The old mindset was that it's better not to know too much about employees. Most presidents of very large companies have no idea what life is like on the shop floor. For them, people are an abstraction, just numbers. But in a small company of, say, 300 or 500 individuals, people are knowable.

Eating together is where personal connections are made. I wanted to see what I could learn by getting to know everyone. Lunch was in groups of about 10 people. This was a critical first step. The idea was to create a point of personal connection: a place of listening and exchange of views where everyone's voice was welcome.

I recall an associate asking to have a photo taken with me during a company event. I said, "Sure." The associate added that her friends didn't believe that she knew and could easily talk with the president of the company. She wanted a picture to prove it and was comfortable explaining why.

I used a natural ritual to craft this cultural event, which extended individual connections. Group lunches—a seemingly small but significant change—were an opportunity for understanding and sharing. Shared meals are natural places to trade stories. Eating together is a bonding ritual. Rituals reinforce culture.

Meaning

Stories embody beliefs. Stories tell us who we are, and what's important. Legends, myths, and parables are a sequence of events that show change over time. While legends aren't factually true, they contain another kind of truth: they convey meaning. Stories stimulate the imagination, speak of emotional truth, make ideas understandable, and communicate direction and hope.

Joseph Campbell explained the meaning and development of life journeys through examination of myth. *The Hero with a Thousand Faces* and *The Power of Myth* are his most famous works. In those, Campbell mapped out the hero's allegorical journey in stages. First, the hero is dissatisfied. He doesn't know much about himself. He is under stress. Then some event happens, a feeling from within, or an external event that calls him to action. He knows he should leave the world of the familiar. He is reluctant to change. Fear of the unknown is just too scary. He refuses the call.

At this point, a mentor appears. One example is Luke Skywalker's meeting with Obi-Wan Kenobi, a Jedi Master in George Lucas's *Star Wars*. Lucas had based the film on Joseph Campbell's work. The mentor teaches the hero and helps him understand himself. Now the hero has the means and courage to cross a boundary into the unknown.

Off he goes. He meets with difficulties to test his mettle. He starts to learn who are his friends and enemies. A greater challenge looms before him. He must now prepare to face his worst fear.

His ordeal results in a symbolic death, but also transcendence. The hero takes on new life. He's won new understanding through the experience of the ordeal. Having won, he is now in danger of losing his prize.

On his way out of the unknown world he meets with enemies jealous of his new-found mastery. Again he is tested by opposing forces. Eventually he returns home to the ordinary world. He is different from the person who started out. He emerges transformed into a higher-level being.

Truth doesn't have to be literal to have practical value. This archetypal hero story shows up in cultures around the world, and has for thousands of years. There must be something to it.

The quest story's real purpose is self-discovery. We find out what we can achieve by doing. As the ancient Chinese philosopher Lao Tzu, who lived from 604 BC to 531 BC, wrote, "A journey of a thousand miles begins with a single step." That single step is a question.

What Do You Want?

You probably have a pat answer to this what-do-you-want question. But it's worth digging deeper, and examining your beliefs. What might you be missing? If you want to consciously change your beliefs, first find out what they are.

If you want to change how your company behaves, first understand what it's doing now.

"What do you want?" is a question that often gets missed because many of us think we're too busy dealing with the pressures of daily life. And this is why it's so important for leaders to go offsite, away from everyday distractions to work on the big questions.

The what-do-you-want question, along with an understanding of your current reality, is the point of beginning. This is where the help of a supportive and experienced coach as ally is a huge help. Coaching conversations have to be confidential, which is why you as leader need a safe and supportive environment to investigate these foundational beliefs.

The value of greater self-awareness is deeper understanding of yourself, other people, and your company. New insight generates new possibilities for action.

In the next chapter we'll describe some effective leadership development tools you can use. It may come as a shock to finally see a gap between how you perceive yourself and how other people see you. This is why privacy is of utmost importance.

Your beliefs about your culture, organizational structure, employees, customers, suppliers, technology, processes, training, may be accurate—or not. But how do you know unless you consciously examine your beliefs? Belief about one area of holistic manufacturing has an effect on all others.

For example, how does your belief about technology affect process, organization, and culture? How do your beliefs about organization impact culture? This examination is an investment.

Let's look at common beliefs manufacturers hold about technology, organization, and culture.

Techno-Belief

In the previous chapter, we described technology as extending to all your tools and know-how required to develop, manufacture, and market products. This includes equipment, processes, and information systems. Many manufacturers don't think about how critical technology is for culture and production.

We won't go into the details of manufacturing technology in this book. In a nutshell, technology helps people do their jobs better. It's an ongoing data bank that houses ever-increasing institutional knowledge. It is a tool that learns. Up-to-date systems need to be in place supporting all of your activities.

Some manufacturers are reluctant to invest in technology. Others will buy top-of-the line systems. Our belief is that there are major problems with both views.

Frugality can hamper your whole operation. Inflexibility, limitations, and lack of comprehensive capabilities will negatively affect processes and output. Time spent fixing and upgrading or creating custom workarounds is rarely figured into the cost of frugal technology. Neither is the opportunity cost of learning a cumbersome system. Frugal technology can end up costing you a bundle.

On the other hand, believing in only the best is usually buying more than you need. One common belief about buying at the top end is that your investment will do everything for you right out of the box. This is rarely the case. Purchasing capacity you'll never use is waste. Many people believe the expensive solution will last a long time. But this is misplaced because technology evolves so rapidly. Planning for two or three years is reasonable. Expecting your current technology to still be effective 10 years from now is unlikely. Predicting a long-term future is almost impossible.

In 1977, Ken Olson, president, chairman, and founder of Digital Equipment Corporation, was of the opinion, "There is no reason anyone would want a computer in their home." Even Bill

Gates predicted Microsoft would never make a 32-bit operating system. Long-term predictions have a greater chance of error the further out you look.

Our practice is to purchase technology in the mid-range, no matter whether it's 3-D printing, a piece of machinery, or an IT system. We believe in the advantage of new technology.

AT was an early adopter of new technologies. We simplified them so they could be implemented. We put everything together in a way that hadn't been done before. The result wildly exceeded everyone's expectations. There's not much point in scheduling every process and every task. Once the system is on the shop floor, it's going to be modified by daily conditions of machinery and people resources. Adapt it so it actually works for what you want to do. Your system needs to be easy to use and as simple as possible. For more details of our strategic implementation of an effective manufacturing system, see pages 131-133 of Richard T. Lilly's book, *The Road to Manufacturing Success, Common Sense throughput Solutions for Small Business.*

You don't have to be tyrannized by your software. It can suck up vast amounts of time for data input you'll never use. Customer Relationship Management (CRM) has been in vogue. Despite its popularity, AT abandoned it because it was too much of an irrelevancy.

The central question is this: What technology do people need to do their jobs better? As we said in the last chapter, a holistic approach integrates technology, culture, beliefs, and organization. All these are artificially defined segments of the whole. In reality they overlap.

In an open organization where associates make rapid, on-the-ground decisions, they need systems that will let them know what's happening in other areas of production. They want to see that there are real-time resources available. They need relevant and accurate information to get the job done.

In a task-oriented culture, one that operates strictly on a need-to-know basis, the technological capabilities you look at will be different. Technology is ultimately a function of culture and organization.

Organizational Belief

Traditional belief about organization is that the only alternative to hierarchical structure is chaos. This is understandable when you have no other experience. And even if it's possible to imagine a flatter and more inclusive organization, now never seems to be the right time to implement. There are always more pressing issues. It's all a matter of belief. As Henry Ford is reputed to have said, "Whether you think you can or can't, you're usually right."

Organization is a structure for product, process, and information flow. We'll have more to say about developing a *process-centered organization* (PCO) in later chapters. PCO is a more flexible structure than traditional task-oriented organizations. A further transition includes PCO and transcends it. This new level is an organic learning culture based on belief in people. Manufacturing must be responsive to the ever-changing global environment.

The future has arrived. Our belief is that responsive organizations are more effective than traditional ones. Such organizations make faster decisions and can rapidly allocate and deploy necessary resources. The promise of a learning culture is sustainable agility. But change doesn't happen overnight.

Urgency and Patience

Here is how it was for us at AT:

AT slowly learned to adapt to market changes, all the time remaining financially stable by controlling growth through steady sales increases and acquisitions.

In November 2001, we implemented our PCO. This significant organizational and cultural transformation followed six years of training for all associates. It took that long to reach a shared understanding and acceptance of what we called "change and challenge." We were forging a new path. We have learned much since, so we don't want to give you the expectation it would take that long to transform your organization. Change is an ongoing process, and it differs for every company.

These days, visitors to AT's plants remark on an atmosphere of productive calm. Frantic shop floor activity is noticeably absent. There's a misguided belief that productivity has to be accompanied by the furrowed brow of concentration, or look like something from an emergency room TV show. This just isn't true. People are more productive when they're less stressed.

Urgency isn't panic. We heard of a taxi driver who put a sign in his taxi: Safety first—poor planning on your part doesn't mean recklessness on mine. John Kotter's *Eight Stages of Change* model continues to influence our thinking. His first step is to create a sense of urgency for change. Without widespread belief in change all else fails.

This means aligning beliefs and securing stakeholder buy-in. Urgency here doesn't mean anxiety-driven frenzy to get product out the door. Urgency is priority.

Urgency and patience may seem like opposites, but the holistic model includes both. You need both a sense of urgency as vital priority, and patience for the long haul. Real growth in a learning organization's culture and capabilities requires patience, nurturing, and care.

AT moved away from a hierarchical decision-making and accountability model (more on these topics later). Instead, we put in place a team-based model, centered on our core processes. The intention was for associates to feel freedom to make and be accountable for their decisions within the context of a supportive culture. Belief in this possibility changed into reality.

Culture Belief

Constant communication keeps your culture alive. A mission statement lost in an office desk does no one any good. Company objectives get written and then forgotten about. Initial enthusiasm doesn't last. When this happens, no one knows what the company's purpose is, and here lies a few dangerous collective delusions.

There are people who believe organizational objectives don't really matter. Or, they are only relevant to a few managers. Company objectives become abstractions, and take second place to the day-to-day running of the company.

Then there is the magical thinking that everyone automatically understands company objectives. They don't. Even worse, there is an overconfident belief that people don't need to know the company's purpose and aspirations. They do.

Successful change from control to collaboration is a process. It can't be imposed without preparation. We will show you how in Chapter 4. For now, the idea is this: any sustainable growth has its roots in belief. Belief is the fuel that drives organizations. And for a belief to be put into practice, it must be spelled out and communicated.

Belief and Commitment

Traditional beliefs are made visible through action. For example, reward for loyal employees has been tenure. Personal sacrifice for the good of the company was part of the package, and security used to be tied to working at just one place. These beliefs are based on an unchanging world.

Contrast these beliefs with a culture where associates are valued for being open to new learning in an atmosphere of rapidly changing demands and the opportunity for contribution to a team. Commitment is a belief.

Loyalty is a reward associates give to the companies they work for. Commitment is not something you can demand of the people in your organization. It is a response. Genuine loyalty comes from appreciation and sometimes even gratitude. Commitment is a freely made choice—a result of positive experience in the workplace.

Manufacturing leaders need clarity and insight. If you believe you're happy, then you probably are. If you believe you're overwhelmed, then that's true, too.

As in the story of the hero, failure to examine your beliefs is to refuse the call for growth. It leaves you vulnerable to self-ignorance, being out of touch, and eventually irrelevant.

In the absence of imagination we only have the past as our guide. We'll say more about leadership vision in the next chapter. Inability to imagine how things could be better limits possibilities. Relying on experience of the past often proves faulty.

According to a Western Union internal memo in 1876, "This 'telephone' has too many shortcomings to be seriously considered as a means of communication. The device is inherently of no value to us." In 1962, Decca Records was quoted as, "We don't like their sound [the Beatles], and guitar music is on the way out." It's comforting to stay with familiar beliefs. But the opportunity cost can be expensive.

Think back to a change of belief in your own life. Have your beliefs really remained the same? Some of them probably have. Like most of us, you continue to believe in death and taxes. Yet which of your beliefs have changed? Do you really still believe in the tooth fairy? You probably did at one time.

Evolving Beliefs

Personal growth—and by extension organizational growth—demands we examine what we believe. The real power of belief is when it generates behavior.

Any action has a potential cost, and so does inaction. You have to make assumptions about the future. All of us do. Being wrong is normal. But what happens when you are wrong? Is it a place for shame and blame or a learning event? Your response depends on your belief.

Our belief is that it is usually better to risk taking action in the long-term direction you imagine. As you step into the fog, you will be able to see farther and adjust along the way. Experience leads to new beliefs, just as beliefs generate new experiences. If you have the courage to explore new horizons;

if you believe you can change, then what sort of future do you want? What change can you imagine?

Belief is a guide to action.

Heartbeat

- Your beliefs drive your actions. Make sure they're in sync.
- Your beliefs set the tone of your company.
- Believe in your employees' creativity.
- Make sure everyone understands your positive beliefs.
- Believe in constant communication.
- Share holistic beliefs with all stakeholders—radiate out.

Chapter Three

Leading from the Heart

He who controls others may be powerful, but he who has mastered himself is mightier still.

—Lao Tzu

Know Yourself First

Winston Churchill wrote that courage is the first of human qualities because it guarantees all others. Researchers discovered that people who display moral courage see themselves as strongly linked to the humanity of other people. Change takes courage.

The word *courage* is derived from the Old French word for heart, *coeur*. Heart is the seat of feeling, so *courage* is heart in action. The ancient *Tao Te Ching* states that courage is derived from love.

You may have noticed love isn't generally what we talk about as manufacturers. But great things happen when people's hearts and minds align. You need to be ready, though, for a reaction when you challenge the status quo. Making this change happen isn't the easiest thing in the world, but it is worthwhile. A sustainable, 21st-century workplace cannot ignore human feeling. Love here isn't romantic mush. Love isn't dropping standards, nor letting people run riot. Love is active care. It's about creating the conditions where people look out for each other and have a common purpose.

Love is an active verb. It's a willingness to help others be their best. A place where people help each other comes from a sense of caring. Care means doing what's right—for everyone.

When people in an organization thrive, so does the organization. Human development has a direct relationship to economic growth because investment in learning expands opportunities, and improves business effectiveness.

The word intuition means learning from within (in-tuition). If you can't understand yourself you haven't much of a chance of understanding other people. Leading requires critical and creative thinking, and being in touch with your intuition: your inner teacher.

Desire to make the world a better place comes from an inner impulse—a feeling. Religious folks have known that impulse as a calling. But you don't need to be religious to feel a passion for doing what you believe is the right thing and believing in a better future. Satisfaction and happiness come from the heart.

There will always be parts of us that are unknowable. Swiss founder of analytical psychology, Carl Jung, developed the concept of the shadow. Most of our impulses and drives are unconscious. According to Jung, everyone has a shadow where irrational impulses and instincts reside. For this reason no human can have full self-knowledge. Assessment tools used by industry today have their roots in Jung's work.

If you can't know yourself completely, you can learn to know yourself better. Another reason for this unknowability is an ever-changing self-perception. Environments are changing all the time. Change calls for new responses. Growth or decline, expansion or contraction is change.

The payoff to better self-understanding is ability to see with greater clarity. You're less likely to fool yourself. You perceive more. You miss less. You gain greater clarity of the needs, desires, and possibilities of people around you. Awareness of what's going on is critical to the success of any organization.

Becoming more aware of how other people respond to you gives you more choices for action. Choice is a kind of wealth. You can practice self-control. You can ask better questions. You can choose how you want to respond to events. Personal experience is the great teacher.

As you develop greater self-clarity, your options expand. You see what was previously hidden. You hear what you've previously been deaf to. It's as if your senses are sharpened. You see, feel, and understand more, with greater depth. What you find may not always be pleasant, but it's more real.

Insight is the act of looking within. Greater awareness means increased sensitivity, and that includes suffering. Yet you now have an opportunity to do something about this suffering. Understanding your preferences—your default biases—grounds you in reality. You can be more effective and open to experiences of greater satisfaction, aliveness, and joy.

The ancient Greek philosopher, Socrates, said, "An unexamined life is not worth living." So how do you begin? The answer is with questions.

Questions

In the last chapter, we introduced the big question: what do you want? Here are more questions to stimulate your thinking:

- What do I care about?
- What do I want to do differently?
- What do I want to learn?
- What do I want to stop doing?
- What sort of people do I want to work with? Most people want to associate with people who share their values because this makes aligning common purpose much easier.
- What sort of environment would bring out my best self? What sort of environment would be better for the whole organization?
- What do I want my company to be?
- How do I regard other people? How do I want to change that?
- What makes me happy?
- What would greater enjoyment look like to me?
- What do I see as making other people happy at work?
- What could I do to make people's private lives better?
- What do I appreciate about the people who work here? What about other stakeholders?
- What do I appreciate about myself?
- What do I think other people appreciate about me?
- How do other people see me?
- How do I want to be different?

- What do I want to build or cultivate?
- What do I want more of?
- What do I want less of?
- What does a good day look like?
- How can things be better? This is the question that never goes away.

We'll have more to say in later chapters about assessment tools to assist with self-understanding.

Patience

An old joke goes that a practicing attorney is one that hasn't got it right yet. But practice is a discipline, a process of continual development. Leadership is a continuous art and not just a means to an end. This idea is thousands of years old. The *Analects* (meaning collection) of Confucius is an ancient Chinese assembly of universal principles dating back some 23 centuries. The *Analects* describes the leader as a patient person, not one to jump to foregone conclusions. That is why leadership is an ongoing practice requiring constant attention. Constant attention is necessary for any practice, whether it's golf, learning a language, or running a manufacturing enterprise. The *Analects* teaches that leadership rests on virtue. Virtue is behavior demonstrating high moral standards.

Confucius wrote that leadership's objective is leadership. It is an art form, the objective is itself. Results are a by-product. The *Analects* has this to say about virtue-based leadership:

He who exercises government by means of his virtue may be compared to the north polar star, which keeps its place and all the stars turn towards it.[1]

---

1   Confucius. *Analects* (Illustrated) (Kindle Locations 165-166). Kindle Edition.

Virtue attracts. The virtue of trust is central to Manufacturing with Heart. We've devoted a whole chapter to it. According to the *Analects*, primary virtues for leadership are patience, trustworthiness, perseverance, knowledge, respect, learning, simplifying, harmony, and wisdom. The ancient book advises reverent attention to business, sincerity, economy in expenditure, love for people, the employment of people at the proper seasons, and importance of ritual and celebration.

Ritual solidifies group values. Thinking about what you value allows you to design a manufacturing culture based on explicit principles. At Manufacturing with Heart, our core principles inform our authentic mission to help people cultivate a positive and productive workplace. Work with Michael Hammer, author of *Reengineering the Corporation*, has influenced our efforts. In a *New York Times* obituary for Mr. Hammer, dated September 4, 2008, author Dennis Hevesi quotes him as writing:

> *I'm saddened and offended by the idea that companies exist to enrich their owners... That is the very least of their roles; they are far more worthy, more honorable, and more important than that. Without the vital creative force of business, our world would be impoverished beyond reckoning.*[2]

From Beliefs to Values

In the last chapter we identified belief as the driver for everything. By examining your beliefs you come to realize what matters to you. Beliefs that matter are values. Of course, not everyone values the same things. Yet within any cohesive group there is significant overlap of values. Think of the center of a Venn diagram. Understanding your own central values, those

---

2   http://www.nytimes.com/2008/09/05/business/05hammer.html

of your community and of other people are essential to lead collective effort. Shared values connect people.

Some values change over time; others are more solid. What we value often changes as we develop. Membership in any values-based group rests upon common understanding, yet values are often in conflict with each other. Personal growth is a process of letting go to make way for something new. A decision today might not be the right decision tomorrow. You have to prioritize values depending on what you want. You may value more revenue, but you may not value what we have to do to get it. Or you may value revenue at any price. Your values shape your world. Decision making is about prioritizing values. Values emerge from two things: beliefs, and conclusions you draw from personal experience.

From Values to Principles

Clarity around values gives you the foundation to form realistic principles. Values are beliefs you care about. Principles are codes of expected behavior. Principles can be shared. Principles are actionable. This is why principles should have their roots in commonly held values.

The principle of the golden rule states that you should treat others in the way you would like to be treated. The idea is reciprocity, and reciprocity is necessary for group harmony.

In the 18th century, the moral philosopher Immanuel Kant wrote about what it is to behave ethically. He was thinking about what is right behavior for anyone. His idea of doing the right thing (moral principle) was that everyone should behave in the same way under the same conditions. He called this the categorical imperative.

For example if you want to be knowledgeable, you must learn. This simple example is true for everyone who wants to gain knowledge. Principle is if you want X, do Y.

As a leader, you can show how it's done. For example, set the standard for the behavior you want. If you want office employees to work from 8 a.m. to 5 p.m., Monday through Friday, be the example. It's the leader's job to set an example. Everyone needs to know you are there.

Everybody knows who is working and who is not, who is sleeping on the job, who always goes above and beyond, who is collaborative and who isn't. The action principle here is to first listen. Understand what's going on, and then respond in positive ways.

When AT worked with CCL, the executive team went offsite for a week of leadership development. Part of this exercise was to take personal assessments and then share strengths AND weaknesses. Butch volunteered first. Gary Rhodes from CCL observed at the time:

From the very beginning, Butch was always willing to go first in terms of sharing things about himself as a way to help other people open up. That really stood out for us [CCL], for it was not something we had seen all that often. At each meeting, someone would say, 'I don't get this, or I'm uncomfortable,' and he would say, 'Well, I'm not comfortable either. I'll get up and let you see what I have.' In our experience, to see that behavior exhibited by a CEO was remarkable.

In such situations when leaders show vulnerability, it makes it a lot less scary for other people to share their 'warts and all'. Vulnerability can be strength. But there are risks to be weighed. It takes guts to be so open. The principle here is that it's OK to be yourself. You can always look for opportunities to demonstrate leadership. What are you demonstrating?

From Principles to Habits

When new principles are accepted they embed in the culture at the organizational level. And at the personal level they are internalized. In other words they become reflexes. For example, looking out for each other becomes a habit based on reciprocity, respect, and shared purpose.

In general, we progress from beliefs to values, from values to principles, and from principles to habits. You can unpack habits and find out what principles, values, and beliefs underlie them.

Identify current habits and ask yourself why they exist. Ask:

- What principles are those habits based on?
- What values underlie existing principles?
- What beliefs form values?
- How do you feel about existing habits?
- Do they serve you?
- Do current habits get in the way?
- Which habits do you want to get rid of?
- Which habits do you want to cultivate?

Seeing the Big Picture

As overall leader, you're responsible for your entire operation. You are well aware that the organization lives in a complex ecosystem. Your manufacturing organization feeds upon raw materials, knowledge, capital, legal and social legitimacy, revenue, labor, and markets. All of these need continual attention. Simplifying is necessary.

Ken Wilber's integral theory continues to influence our thinking. Wilber writes that the holon integrates various points of view.

In Chapter One, we described the holon as being a complete thing in itself and also a member of a larger whole. An atom is a complete entity and part of a molecule. A molecule is part of a cell, and so on.

Here is a simple way to think about holons at work. Individuals work in a manufacturing company. Each individual is part of a team. Each team is part of a larger group. All groups together make up the whole which is in this example the company. Your company is a thing in itself. But it's also part of a greater whole, the manufacturing industry.

Each of these holons is a complete system in itself. Each has a different perspective. Each one integrates into larger wholes. Complex systems are built upon simple holonic structures, which provide stability.

Wilber writes of holonic perspectives as an alternative to what he calls a dominator hierarchy: the authoritarian model. Wilber's work is vast in scope. He's authored some 20 books—a number of them the thickness of a house brick. His work picks up where Maslow left off—and then some.

Beyond self-actualization, the apex of Maslow's *hierarchy of needs*, lays the spiritual domain of self-transcendence. But we're not going that far in this book. Wilber's great contribution to business is his *AQAL* model.

What follows is a simplification of an immense, far reaching, and complex topic. AQAL stands for All Quadrants All Levels. In its simplest form it looks like this:

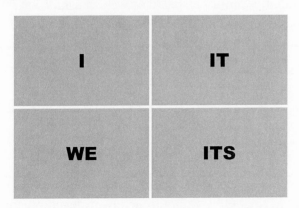

At the top left is the "I" quadrant. This is your *interior individual perspective or awareness.*

Below it is the "WE" quadrant: *how you feel inside and experience in relation to another person or group.*

The "IT" quadrant is your *awareness of objective reality*—experience generated from your physical surroundings.

The bottom right is "ITS", a *group perspective of objective reality*, for example, a collective point of view of a complete manufacturing plant, or consensus on the usefulness of a particular material.

The top row of the model, "I" and "IT" are *individual perspectives*. The bottom row of the model, "WE" and "ITS" are *collective perspectives.*

On the left column "I" and "WE" are *interior or subjective perspectives*. On the right "IT" and "ITS" are *objective, or agreed upon points of view.*

A point of view is what you can see from where you are. So where are you? This model helps answer that question.

Taking these four perspectives we can ask. What does [you fill in the blank] mean to me? What does it mean to us?

What does it mean to me?	How do I become it?
How do we talk about it?	How do we become it?

The "L" in AQAL refers to levels of development. In this example, we'll use the bottom right quadrant: external objective. The objective reality of a company may be at any developmental level.

Let's look at four levels in the ITS quadrant:

1. A start-up company, or one with serious problems, may focus entirely on survival. Roles aren't yet defined. It's all hands to the pumps. Putting-out-fires management means we shall see chaos and drama. No one is in any doubt about this external objective reality.

2. A higher level organization is bureaucratic. Now there is order. Following procedures matters most. Change happens slowly. The focus is inward. Everyone knows that it has to be done by the book.

3. Higher still is a flexible organization that values challenging the rules. What the bureaucratic organization above sees as punishable deviation, this level of development calls creativity. The buzzword is disruption. The bureaucratic organization is

authoritarian; this one is political. Self-expression, influence, and initiative are positive, but taken too far can lead to narcissism, arrogance, and lack of direction. Cats are notoriously hard to herd. Leading such an organization requires more from a leader than rank.

4. Leadership in even more-developed organizations will see itself in the role of steward, mentor, and servant. "Systems thinking" is the norm. People experience enjoyment at work. Communication is a finely honed capability. Interpersonal relationships support collaboration and the company's mission. This is the culture of trust, care, and effectiveness.

As development progresses, each new level encompasses and transcends the previous one. Under stress there is the impulse to revert to an earlier developmental stage. If you have children, you understand this well. Stress tends to cause defensive reactions and withdrawal. Lower levels of development have fewer choices. As a company matures it has more options for behavior. This is also true for people.

Environment and experience shape perspectives. A task is a fragment. A process is a whole. The legacy of 18th century philosopher Adam Smith remains with us today. He rejected process and promoted the idea of task specialization. The idea stuck until the 1980s, when a shift in perspective caused U.S. industry to begin reengineering itself. Leaders need to hone awareness of this kind of cultural climate change. Large-scale shifts in perspective have far-reaching consequences.

Task and process are two fundamentally different points of view. This idea is central to a *process-centered organization* (PCO). When people's jobs become more thought-provoking, demanding, and varied, opportunities for leadership open up at all levels.

69

Leadership at Any Level

At the heart of process-centering are people and the work they perform. Anyone can share what they know by helping someone else expand their knowledge and skill. Willingness to assist others is dependent on organizational chemistry and climate.

At AT, we flattened the organizational chart. The term "associate" became the name for all people working for the company. We have more to say about renaming and its impact on people and organizational climate in the next chapter. The important point here is that every associate can have an opportunity to lead. A leader is a teacher, and a good teacher speeds up progress. The roles within our flattened structure look like this:

1. Business process engineer (CEO or business owner)

2. Leadership: process engineers and coaches

3. Team members

An Associate may have more than one role depending on their skills and the needs of the company.

Process engineers and coaches form a dual leadership model for each process. The difference is in their primary focus which is leadership. (*See Appendix: Manage vs. Lead*)

Process engineers define and monitor processes. They're responsible for throughput, productivity, cost, and quality. At the same time, they're balancing the needs of associates, the company, and customers. They have a holistic understanding of the activities of the company.

Largely through technology they can monitor other teams and help where necessary. Their flexible role is to teach processes and specific tasks and to support team members. They work with coaches to define and maintain individual associate development plans, help resolve conflicts, and develop long-term process training. Boundaries between coaches and process engineers are permeable.

Coaches counsel, support, build relationships, inspire, educate, mentor, discipline when needed, and provide training for associates. Similar to process engineers, coaches need a holistic understanding of the business, its needs, its processes, and strategic direction.

Coaches support associates as they implement short- and long-term objectives. They are responsible for HR compliance and balancing the time of associates working in multiple processes. They hire and assign people to process teams.

Intention

Everyone needs some sense of the big picture. Communicating a general understanding of the business and what it's trying to achieve supports common purpose. Intention is a compass point.

In the absence of a restrictive, rule-bound culture, constantly communicating your general direction opens up the conversation for responses of how to get there. In a complex system, parts change all the time. People create a collaborative environment when hearts and minds resonate in harmony.

With leaders in every level of a holistic manufacturing company, associates should be or become interdependent collaborators. Interdependence is an idea worth some explanation. Assessment tools based on Susanne Cook-Greuter's *leadership maturity framework* (LMF) helped us understand a progression

71

of human development from dependent to independent to interdependent.

Assessments can identify strengths so people are assigned to work they're interested in and/or capable of. Interest is the springboard to knowledge. Assessment tools can show areas that are less developed, too. This is not a bad thing. It's a potential learning opportunity. When you know the direction you want to move toward, it shapes the kinds of questions you ask.

Curiosity energizes. Desire to learn means you're receptive.

There are many versions of the following story: A scholar wanted to know more about wisdom. He went to a master, who offered him tea. The scholar accepted and eagerly anticipated his drink. The scholar held out his cup and the master poured tea. But he kept on pouring until the cup overflowed. Alarmed, the scholar cried, "Stop! The tea cup is too small. You're wasting tea." The master explained that the tea cup is like the mind. You need room for new knowledge.

We know today that the mind isn't limited in this way. However, the story illustrates that letting go of outmoded viewpoints is as important as adopting new ones. Receptivity means willingness to look at existing assumptions and have the courage to let them go when they're no longer useful.

Leading a holistic manufacturing company requires multidimensional awareness. Your ability to play various roles allows you to make connections at every level of your organization. You become like an actor who wakes up in the mornings asking, "Who am I today?" This doesn't mean you're insincere; quite the opposite. Sincerity is a fundamental attribute of leading from the heart.

Your choice of behavior depends on the situation. Sometimes you need to be a teacher, a specialist, or a freethinker. Sometimes you have to be the messenger of bad news. This is always a tough one for every leader, but is a perfect place to demonstrate care.

Fierce competition forced changes in our plant in Mexico. First, we reduced the workday. Eventually, we had to cut payroll by 30 percent. In September of 2012, despite every effort to keep people in the company, AT Carbide de México began to close the plant. A former associate of the company, C.B., tells it this way:

We always had support and resources. He [Butch] taught us by example, just being there, working, speaking with us, to such an extent that when he was absent, we would ask ourselves, "What would Butch do to address this issue?" We gave thanks for the opportunity of being part of this unique and special company.

Despite the Mexico setback, AT continues to successfully operate nine locations around the world. Leading from the heart aspires to more than value for owners or shareholders.

Developing

Ken Wilber sees human consciousness as evolving. As more people access advanced levels of personal experience, they no longer are willing to react to structures created at lower levels. They want to create more humane and civilizing environments.

When enough leaders operate at a higher level we will have reached a tipping point. It's taken us about a million and a half years to evolve since early man first walked upright. Humans invented agriculture twelve thousand years ago. Today, technology is advancing at a dizzying rate. But our biology evolves slowly. Our emotional responses have not caught up with the world we find ourselves in. We are biologically hard-wired to think and act in the short term.

Our next evolution must be conscious if we are to survive as a species. This responsibility is with every individual. Each of us has to be accountable for our own development. The good news is that humans are adaptable. If we weren't, we wouldn't have survived this long. Leadership at every level is limited or expanded by an individual's ability to improve awareness and learn in all directions. This is the never-ending work.

Sincerity is the key to connecting with hearts and minds of other people. Communicate with everyone, letting them know their value to the company and to you personally. It's crucial to be genuine. People know when they're being hoodwinked. Sincerity is not a manipulative technique, but comes from feeling. And it's feeling that ultimately motivates people. Actions demonstrate intention.

Developmental potential is within everyone. Development is unfolding through stages. Just as a child first crawls, then stands, then walks, and finally runs, developing is unfolding of possibility and potential. Your own new developing state can be the springboard for creating higher levels of organizational reality.

Presence

Our AT sessions with Susan Cook-Greuter started with an exercise of quiet reflection (mindfulness), where for just two minutes group participants concentrated on watching their breathing. This helped us center our awareness to be more present.

The mindfulness technique is simply to focus on breathing in and breathing out. Notice how concentration gets sidelined by mental chatter; what you'd been doing before the meeting, what you're doing after. Notice what's going on, and then bring attention back to the breath.

Calm can be cultivated. Unruffled effectiveness is what visitors to AT often remark upon. Recognition came in 2008 when AT received a regional Best Places to Work award. A caring and effective culture comes from the developmental work of its CEO or business owner, and then by extension development through leaders at every level.

In an airplane emergency, you know the drill. Put on your own oxygen mask before you turn to help someone else. Taking care of yourself means you have more to give.

You've probably seen these ads in the business press. There's a picture of someone with a pair of binoculars looking into the distance. Somewhere in the title is "vision." But the danger in this concept is that the person who's looking through the binoculars may be quite unaware of what's going on where he's standing. Being present to what is happening right here, right now matters.

You do need to make guesses about the future, but you're not going to see much with those binoculars beyond clouds or fog. The further out you look the fuzzier the picture. As we said above, intention drives action. Developing sensitivity to what's happing now is where options for practical action lie.

The first step is right here in this moment. This step could be small. Once you've made it, look around. What's changed? Then ask yourself:

- What do we have here?

- What's at stake?
- What's now possible?
- Are connections among groups and individuals strengthened or weakened?
- Are people collaborating or competing?
- What obstacles can I remove?
- What's coming to life?
- What's dying?
- What is the emotional temperature of this new place?
- How are people helping each other?
- How is the entire system behaving?
- What have you been doing that you've been previously unaware of?
- How risky is this new situation?
- How do I feel about that?
- How are other people reacting to a new situation?
- How am I supporting a new change?
- How am I going to sustain it?
- What could I be missing here?
- What do I do next?

Those questions come from being highly aware of what is going on in the present moment. Everything you do is in this unique moment. Leading from the heart demands a wholesale change of culture. This means an examination of values, and openness to personal and organizational change.

Life Is an Experiment

No one knows what the future may bring. But always operating from the heart's higher states knocks down barriers and creates new, more functional practices. As we said above, leadership is a practice. It never ends. There is always room for growth. Experimenting takes courage. But what are the alternatives? You can unlock human ingenuity and spirit, in yourself and in others.

As a leader you prepare the ground. Bringing self-development tools into the workplace gives people a chance to experience themselves in new ways. Be warned—learning burns calories. It's energy-intensive. When you learn something new, you are actually changing your anatomy. You grow connective material in the brain. Because you model behavior as a leader, you need adequate rest for renewal. Remember work/life balance.

Learning patience for action-oriented leaders doesn't come naturally. But patience is a virtue and for any long journey with inevitable bumps in the road, you need it. Patience is never absolute, but is expandable. With intention guiding direction, patience helps you endure the necessary setbacks of life's tests.

How did AT manage to change from command and control? How did it meet resistance and make positive change happen? Turn the page to find out.

Heartbeat

- Know yourself: leadership is based on values. Be clear about what they are.
- Be patient, especially with yourself.
- Invest in your self-development first.
- Everyone can practice the art of leadership.
- Leadership is an ongoing practice, not a means to an end.
- Observe what is. Stop, look, listen. See from multiple perspectives: AQAL
- Cultivate harmony. Check for alignment of values with principles, and identify habits.
- Simplify as much as you can, but not too much
- Demonstrate care. Smooth the path, remove obstacles.

Chapter Four

Shift Happens

I remember the sales meeting when Butch became the first Process Engineer. He announced, "The boat is turning left. And if you're not onboard, it's perfectly alright, but we're going that way." That way was the way of the process-centered organization. That really stuck with me. The company is almost self-sustaining because of it. I have a degree in business management and I thought, 'Man alive, where he's headed to is probably the most efficient and cost-effective way to run a company anywhere.

—Customer Communications, Sales - AT

Toward an Entirely New Structure

In the beginning, we didn't even know what leadership was or what it meant. The first thing we did was learn about leadership for ourselves. It all started with Myers–Briggs Type Indicator (MBTI®). Self-awareness began to unfold, then global awareness, then spiritual awareness. Learning just keeps going.

TANYA: After eight years of groundwork, Butch was ready to move to the next level. We'd worked that long to understand team building and change management with CCL. Before our annual spring meeting in 2001, Butch asked the leadership staff to prepare by reading Hammer's *Reengineering the Corporation*.

Butch's vision was to use everything we had worked on to create and implement a significant change in our organizational structure. He wanted a much flatter organization. One where associates felt more connected to their contributions, decision making, and the outcomes of the business. He wanted to build upon Hammer's concepts and process-organization framework to create an entirely new structure.

What did this mean? We had no idea. We talked for hours about the possibilities. And still left feeling unbalanced. It was like treading water in a pool without edges. Only later did we realize how the company was evolving from machine to an intelligent living organism.

I could hear CCL's John McGuire's words: "If you don't feel uncomfortable, you're not making progress with change effort." According to John, we were making great progress.

***

Job security is a top priority for working people. Introducing radical new ideas can be disconcerting. Routine gives you the impression of safety. You know what you're doing. You don't have to think too much. You feel capable. Routine makes life easier. But change disrupts exiting patterns. Necessary disruption can leave folks feeling angry, confused, and anxious.

BUTCH: I was in a meeting with one of our associates, Mike. We were talking about Eli Goldratt's *The Goal*. We discussed how each person has to be aware of the whole process. They need to look in front and look in back. They have to plan on what they're doing rather than just keep making stuff independently of what's happening. It makes no sense to keep making parts we can't use and nobody wants. You only need inventory of raw materials or something very basic.

Mike said, "You're telling me that if I'm really efficient then I should basically stop, sit down, and do nothing?"

"That's right," I said. "You're better off sitting on your hands than continuing to use up resources making parts for inventory."

Then I went on to explain, "No, I don't want you sitting there doing nothing. There is a job somewhere to be done."

I told him, "If your job is done, then go somewhere else. You have the freedom to move. Go make that happen. You need to figure out how to make parts now, when the order comes in. Your driver is parts out the door. Each specific order determines what's made. If you're prepared to make the order when it comes in, then you don't have to have finished goods inventory."

The Goal

Real teamwork kicks in when people understand the holistic process. Previously unnoticed inefficiencies come to light. This results in more customer satisfaction. When associates learn to identify and address constraints, the effectiveness of the organization increases. This is why we had everyone read or listen to the audio version of *The Goal*.

The Goal: A Process of Ongoing Improvement, by Eliyahu Goldratt and writing partner Jeff Cox, appeared in 1984. The book has now sold over 2 million copies. It's written as a novel charting the course of people in a complex manufacturing business who come to understand how business processes work.

The story is told from the perspective of fictional character Alex, the plant manager. As the book opens, he's in a miserable situation. Business is unprofitable. Parts out the door are always late. On top of that, he's given only three months to turn things around. This stress affects Alex's home life, too.

Jonah, a physicist, who many believe to be a stand-in for Goldratt, teaches Alex concepts by posing questions rather than instructions. In this way, Alex and his team learn to figure out things for themselves.

Along the way, Alex comes to understand dependent events and the need to free resources so they can be allocated somewhere else.

Goldratt's *theory of constraints* (TOC) underlies the book's message. Obstacles are referred to as bottlenecks. Bottlenecks show up in a number of ways: for instance, ineffective technology, alienating policy, or lack of ongoing employee development. Identifying and reducing these limiting bottlenecks becomes an ongoing priority. Alex's perspective undergoes a change. The book ends with him looking at what to change, how to make it happen, and what to change into.

What to change into? That was the question for us.

Imagining Our Future

TANYA: We imagined learning spreading beyond production processes. What if we addressed complex emotional issues all of us humans have to navigate? What about adding practical education such as how to enjoy working together? What if we all learned to communicate better, and how to listen respectfully? Could we balance work and life for greater satisfaction?

"Have fun" became one of our expectations. We slowly put in place what we call Manufacturing with Heart.

From Titles to Freedom

At one time, there had been 47 vice presidents, managers, supervisors and foremen at AT. Our new leadership team was comprised of eight process engineers and eight coaches. As we made our organization flatter we removed the titles. That was when we saw how deeply hierarchical thinking permeated everything, not just business, but the outside culture as well.

For example, a foreman would feel disadvantaged because he was now simply an associate. His status had rested upon eight people reporting to him. Suddenly, he thought he was a nobody. Maybe his neighbor was just promoted to supervisor. How could our associates maintain self-esteem without a recognizable title? People were feeling the ground shifting beneath their feet.

Gradually, associates figured out what they could tell their friends and neighbors. It went something like this: "I don't have a boss. I have a broader playing field than you have."

Talk about titles shifted to pride in the organization. This was much more fulfilling. Those competitive discussions of social status turned to our associates' advantage. Instead of, "My boat's bigger than your boat," they could say, "Yeah, I have a yacht." The switch to "no boss" flipped the conversation. People figured out they could talk about something other than their title. Then associates became top dog. Now their friends wanted to know more about the company and how it worked.

People throughout the company were noticeably happier. They began owning their own significance and contribution. So people started to change. Associates' hearts and minds opened as they came to recognize and use their unique talents.

We encouraged associates to share information and ideas about improvement. No longer were all ideas and innovations expected to come from the top. We put in place cross-training so associates could understand how the organization operated and how it functioned in the wider world. We encouraged them to ask questions so they could broaden their thinking about their own work.

Know the Why

AT went through a period of intense growth, acquiring nine companies in three countries in seven years. We needed to integrate these companies, people, and processes. The first thing we did was describe our vision of growth for the future. We wanted everyone to share in the excitement of new possibilities we were collectively creating. We communicated values and the principles driving AT's activities.

Sharing purpose let associates know where they stood. Everyone's holistic understanding deepened and this allowed greater tolerance for change.

BUTCH: As a clear sign things were changing for the better, we provided common telephone and computer systems, and improved the cafeteria and restroom facilities. It was amazing how doing these simple things changed everyone's perspectives during stressful times of acquisitions and mergers.

An energizing ripple effect spread throughout the organization. People talked with each other. They came to trust in the strength and resilience of their organization. Associates started to enjoy themselves at work much more. That created a new and positive workplace climate. Conflict lessened. Cooperation increased.

We constantly shared big-picture goals for the company. Associates understood why they were being asked to do certain things. As trust became common, people started coming up with creative solutions to workplace problems.

When everyone understands "the why," people can make their own choices whether it's the direction they want to go in— or not. There will always be outliers. Some people will resist change. They need to find a more suitable environment. But our investment in communication and openness met with approval for the vast majority of people who chose to grow with us.

Our mantra became: If we're all in, we all win.

Understanding

Part of being "all in" meant continual learning for everyone. Our leadership team came to understand from experience with Michael Hammer's work the challenge we had given ourselves

Reengineering the Corporation, by Michael Hammer and James Champy, was first published in 1993. It offered a new way for corporations to replace processes, organization, and culture inherited from the 19th century.

The central theme of the book was improving outdated processes. Eventually, the revolutionary idea became to place people at the center of organizations. Moreover, they should be treated with respect and trust.

Hammer's big idea was to reverse the Industrial Revolution. There were two main problems. First, successful implementation stumbles when management itself is unwilling to change. Second, failure to shift happens when corporations don't commit to holistic cultural change. This kind of change remains a difficulty for large enterprises. But we were eager to venture into new territory. Our curiosity drove us on. We committed ourselves to improving an already financially successful enterprise. We understood process is a group of tasks that generate customer value. And value-added work is work customers are willing to pay for. Waste, such as making parts just for inventory, is unnecessary.

Associates were asked to read or listen to books so they could make sense of what was happening. Many thought reading books, or listening to them, was something to be done outside of work. This was because of the old definition of work as limited to making product. Yet, the definition of work came to encompass much more. Some associates were surprised that reading at work was just as important as making parts. People came to understand that learning is the work.

The old process was linear: each stage dependent on the next. Like a chain with a weak link, the system was vulnerable. The new process orientation added a robust hub-and-spoke model. The question became not who is doing what, but who should be doing what?

Redefining and expanding roles meant we needed to understand more about the people who worked at the company. People needed to know more about themselves. What were their preferences? What were their capabilities? What did they want to do?

We asked associates to step up and take risks. They did—and they still do. We wanted them to be curious and expand their knowledge. We encouraged them to find joy in learning. AT invested resources to make all this happen.

Learning for Everyone

Everyone took the MBTI in half-day training classes to learn about communication preferences.

Off-site meetings remove distractions of the normal work day so people can share their thoughts, fears, and hopes. We invested in basic communications classes so associates could become aware of body language and improve their ability to listen. Some groups attended negotiations seminars.

Situation Behavior Impact Model (SBI) became our preferred tool for learning to communicate difficult messages without judgment. The model asks first for a description of a situation. The idea is to be as specific as possible in your observations about what, where, and when. The next step, behavior, is to avoid judgment. Rather than interpreting behavior the idea is to describe observed facts. The last step is impact, what you experience from the event.

We held small discussion groups centered upon *The Goal* so everyone had a chance to ask questions and share ideas. Understanding and communication improved through greater participation in team meetings. People got involved in cross-process training. We started an apprentice program. Interested associates could try out machinist positions. We added a customer service apprenticeship program. This gave folks in manufacturing an opportunity experience an office job.

TANYA: Everyone was given an opportunity, but if it didn't work out they could take their old job back. Most importantly, people got a chance to change and learn something new if they had the desire.

The new mindset gave people the idea of continual improvement. Everyone in the company came to understand the value of customer satisfaction improvement, shortening manufacturing cycle time, and searching for opportunities to reduce costs.

Flexing

We started a peer review initiative for process teams. The idea was give associates useful feedback. We asked coaches to get peer reviews from three of five associates who worked with an individual and then integrate them into a single review form. We had no idea how much of a challenge this was going to be. In the end, it became clear that people were reluctant to provide information on their co-associates. Some refused. We saw there was too much intimidation and fear. So eventually we eliminated reviews altogether.

We learned the importance of understanding the current situation before making any changes. Previously, pay for associates had been tied to past performance. We were reaching for something new, which resulted in individual associate development plans. We surveyed everyone. We wanted to understand thoughts and feelings about the current pay-for-past-performance review process.

Before presenting our plan, the developmental team kicked the idea around. How should we respond to resistance? We talked it through and came to unanimous agreement. Individual associate development would embody our positive, progressive learning culture, and the new initiative worked.

Our internal positive culture extends to suppliers, customers, industry, and community. We felt we'd done a good job when AT was recognized as one of the best places to work in Central Ohio by *Columbus Business First* newspaper. We didn't want to stop here, though. We continued to tweak the system.

Job definitions and organizational structures became flexible. People got it: values and beliefs matter. We encouraged thinking and planning at every level. We asked more questions. Was everything we were doing necessary? We thought about it.

Many times, we realized we were doing things we no longer needed. But more than that, we now questioned our own ideas at the planning stage. So apart from getting rid of things, maybe we didn't need to do them in the first place.

TANYA: I gradually realized that our complex attendance policy generated a lot of distrust. Taking this on seemed like a perfect place to make significant change. I was shocked to see that we had 20 pages of policy. And that was just for time off. The details were mindboggling. Not to mention all the wasted time for supervisors and HR associates trying to track everything. No one was ever fired due to attendance policy anyway. I was determined we could do better.

We did the unthinkable. After a couple of years of study and negotiation we scrapped our attendance policy. A We replaced it with what we call an attendance guideline. This simple guideline captured the essence of our belief: You don't need a lot of rules when people want to contribute and you trust them.

BUTCH: We were creating a trust-based system. If you say "we trust you," and put in the system that says "I don't trust you," then people don't understand what's going on. You can't say I trust you and at the same time say I'm going to clock you in every minute, going to monitor everything you do, I'm going to follow you around and write it all down.

TANYA: If you only have sick days and someone needs a day off, associates have to lie. Then people have to break rules. Managers were put in a position of judging good or not good enough reasons not to be at work. It doesn't have to be that way.

***

Clarity

AT's attendance guidelines became simple and clear:

- Be at work on time for scheduled hours
- Schedule needed time off with your team
- Record your hours worked
- Report unscheduled time off immediately to your team

At first associates were puzzled. They were skeptical about the new policy. They kept looking for the "gotcha!" It took a long time for them to see we were sincere. When they understood our intention, they showed appreciation and gratitude. People no longer had to lie if they needed personal time off.

We wanted a shared understanding of the holistic view. As an agile company immediately responding to customer requests, people had to see what was happening everywhere in real time.

And then another mind-changing concept was introduced: We now started thinking about using more systems and less paper. This really kicked in when we implemented our Visual Manufacturing System. All associates could see orders, operations steps, and reports from computers rather than from paper. This was a big step in developing transparency and accessibility of information for everyone. Its value paid off. People were able to make better decisions about process and products.

We surveyed customers for what they wanted to learn about us. We stripped out unnecessary language. In its place, we described our unique ways of satisfying customers' needs.

AT's Business Process Manual conveys clarity of vision. It works on multiple levels. Associates use it as a written framework for our PCO. Each process engineer contributed content to this living documentation. We constantly look for ways to incorporate new processes and simplify them.

We learned that inflexible or large-scale planning is doomed to fail. We took baby steps, and watched to see what happened. Then we could respond effectively. Our leadership team kept their eye on the prize: a culture where people want to come to work.

Transforming Ourselves as Leaders

Intense leadership growth spread throughout the company. We held monthly leadership development meetings.

Three tools we'd used with CCL helped us connect, communicate, and understand ourselves as individuals and as a group: Dialogue, Visual Explorer, and Putting Something in the Middle. We explored together how we could deal with ambiguity and the very necessary state of "not yet knowing."

Experience with these tools showed us how to work as a group instead of compete individually. We could share ideas, instead of defend them. But this required us to look at our assumptions instead of debate them. We went beyond I am right and you are wrong. We learned to put our assumptions on hold, listen to other voices, and see value in what they have to say.

Suspending judgment is not easy for anyone. It's counter-intuitive. After all, no one wants to look like a fool, especially in front of peers. Creating a space where individuals wouldn't be put down was therefore important from the beginning. These experiences allowed for team members to take a second look at their assumptions in a safe place. The group transitioned from a collection of individual opinions and occasionally defensive viewpoints to shared understanding, inclusiveness, and greater possibilities.

These guiding principles emerged:

TILL — teamwork, information, learning, language

DEPENDABILITY — trustworthy, reliable, responsible

INITIATIVE — energetic, enthusiastic, self-motivated

LEADERSHIP — ambitious, daring, experienced, persuasive

JOB KNOWLEDGE — knows and performs job responsibilities

PRODUCTIVITY — works smarter, faster, better

QUALITY — performs with distinction

New Developments

One result of our collective shift in perspective was what we look for in hiring. No longer did we just look for a person with specific skills. Instead we looked for a fit, a sense of passion, ability to collaborate and understand a process-centered organization, desire to learn and succeed. Regardless of the position, we looked for people who wanted to be part of and add to something great.

We continued to support and communicate new initiatives:

- Continual learning for everyone
- Profit sharing, and incentive compensation for team excellence
- Ongoing product and process development
- Support for long-term decision making
- Productivity boost through general understanding of concepts in *Reengineering the Corporation* and *The Goal.*
- Leadership development and change management with Center for Creative Leadership

TANYA: We wanted to get rid of the old notions of human resources. We kept the legal requirements and now included supportive coaching. Our new name for this process became Associate Development and Resources (AD&R).

I was amazed by the collaborative effort of the AD&R team. Our four-day, off-site meeting was the most fulfilling experience of my 25 years with AT.

We understood that constant change was the norm. Instead of working against it, we could be at peace within ourselves— even during periods of chaos. If people were going to learn they had to have the desire to do so. And we would encourage this through an open, motivating and supportive environment.

Self-direction would replace surveillance. Cross-learning would become a habit. New ideas emerged to make processes work together seamlessly. We committed to working toward a new culture that would be a comfortable and fun place to work. The result: a fresh perspective for the future.

Language

TANYA: The word *employee* had always sounded servile to Butch. He didn't want anyone to feel that way. Employees became "associates." He wanted people to feel part of a productive group, passionate about getting work done and sharing in the rewards. We decided to list the traits of an AT associate [*See Appendix*]. These were the first of many new definitions which would come with the creation of the process-centered organization.

Language was critical to the transformation of associates' attitudes and behaviors. Take the expression "eight and hit the gate." Eight hours and you're out of there doesn't embody motivation and enjoyment. Just changing language isn't going to change things if everything else stays the same. In order to change, you need to be sensitive to the words you use.

Words matter. Words carry baggage, and leaders should know what that baggage is. Take the word "mistake". It is an action taken in error, but it also carries emotional baggage.

During my first months with Butch, I recall sitting at my computer and struggling with a response letter to one of our distributors. He was disgruntled about something we had done, a late delivery or a bad product. This customer was upset enough to write a letter directly to the "president." I was probably groaning, which I've been known to do from time to time. Butch came in and asked what was troubling me. I explained.

He scanned the letter and simply said, "Well, it seems like you're trying to skirt around the truth. Just be honest." I sat there for a moment. With a big sigh of relief and tears in my eyes, I created the letter, apologized for our shortcoming, and explained what we would do so it wouldn't happen again.

***

A mistake for one person is a shameful event. It could evoke fear of punishment. For another person a mistake is the necessary result of trial and error, a learning event on the path to greater awareness.

Another example of how words carry emotional baggage is in the want ads. You've probably seen companies looking for aggressive salespeople. What does this language say? Someone who will argue with customers? Someone who will snarl and bite them in the leg? What's trying to be communicated is a request for someone who shows enthusiasm, initiative and persistence. Language reflects worldview.

Western culture has traditionally valued the outstanding individual rather than the whole group. We've inherited this individualistic mindset. Individual achievement in school is praised rather than group effort. Sports teams have stars, but without supporting members they couldn't shine.

Individual competitiveness is a survival instinct, and one we share with just about every living creature. But cooperation is also necessary to survival. We humans are social animals. To be part of a group we have to modify our individualistic urges. We have to do some thinking.

You've heard the competitive language: My boat is bigger than your boat. I win, you lose. This sort of one-upmanship is nothing new. It's been going on for thousands of years. The ancient Greeks had the same issues. And they were the ones who invented democracy.

Individualism is a starting point. People naturally own ideas and opinions and want to defend them. The question is do existing structures support the individual at the expense of the group? Sharing in Western culture may feel uncomfortable—at least at first.

In conformist cultures like Japan's, standing out from the crowd is shameful. It disrespects the group. People in rigid hierarchies are discouraged from asking questions, so information only flows in one direction. This is a stumbling block to innovation. It doesn't tap into collective know-how. Isolated individualism and conformist subservience are extremes. But they are both inheritances. They both need to be recognized for what they are.

Individuals can learn to become comfortable participating in collective effort. Given the right environment the subservient person can risk visibility and individual contribution. People need a safe place to try different behaviors, and our social norms are influenced by the language we use.

TANYA: Butch coined the slogan: "change and challenge." He had this on business cards at AT. He congratulated and acknowledged folks when they made a big change for themselves or their process. He used it to encourage those who were struggling with change.

It served as a gentle reminder that things change all the time, from our customers to the world around us. It is also a precursor for good things to come. This concept helped us work from a realistic, prepared mindset.

Words weave our primary web of connection. "I" become "We." At AT, we determined our language would convey respect, care, clarity, and the enjoyment of working together. But there is more to life than work.

Beyond the Workplace

Remember the question: What do you want? For us at AT, it was about running a successful business that would offer employees enough money to raise their families, a sense of meaning and enjoyment in a productive work environment, and a place for everyone to grow.

It took time to convince some of our associates that we were serious about work-life balance. We firmly believe that work hours need to be limited. There's data to prove it. Productivity goes down as workers put in long hours.

In a recent paper, John Pencavel of Stanford University showed that reducing very long working hours increases productivity.[1] Reasonable working hours may boost productivity, but there is another compelling reason. People need time to have a life outside of work. Apart from rest and renewal, family, personal, and community life all need nurtured. That requires an investment of time and energy.

BUTCH: If someone is working long hours on a regular basis, they're either not competent to do their job or they've been given, or have taken on too much. For workaholics, I would just turn off their lights and tell them to go home. We were clear about expected work hours for exempt and non-exempt associates. Some non-exempt people like overtime work for the extra money. We said, "No."

We don't support long hours. It's not because of cost to the company. We want associates to have plenty of time away from work. People have children and parents who need them. This benefits associates, the company, and therefore the customer. Doing the right thing for dedicated associates is more important.

There is a concept called Five Hundred Leaders. The ideal is to have everyone a leader. Five hundred leaders isn't quite a reality yet at AT, but we've made huge progress. Greater freedom means people are more relaxed, comfortable, and less stressed.

1   http://ftp.iza.org/dp8129.pdf

Initially some people abused their new-found liberty, but that's no reason to go backward.

Take the attendance policy. On the front-end, some people did abuse it. They constituted a tiny minority. Once you give freedom, it's sort of like sending a high school kid off to college. It was just a handful who misused it, but then everybody wanted to put back in rules and regulations. I said, "No. Let's deal with these few people." Everyone knew who they were, so we coached the outliers.

Lowering Stress

People appreciate not having a manager, supervisor, or foreman looking over their shoulder. When people are treated as adults, wellbeing improves and stress decreases. The result is more productive focus. Being trusted and respected gives people the freedom to do the job they think has to be done without feeling nervous. No one wants to be treated like a robot.

If associates leave the company for another job, someone will be looking over their shoulder. They know that. We've often heard it said: "Here I don't feel beat upon. I don't feel somebody's taking advantage of me, so I'm staying here."

Treating people well creates emotional connection and loyalty. But the reason we do it is that it's the right thing to do.

Visitors to AT remark on seeing people working hard yet not seeming stressed. Our culture stimulates wellbeing. We have wellness programs, but it's the culture of care, trust, and respect that actively promotes lowering stress.

In the last three years our health insurance bill has gone down substantially. Two things caused this: Number one, people are healthier. At the same time, people are making better judgments. We've talked a lot about health at AT. Associates have health insurance and we want them to use it. We want them to go to the doctor. We tell them: If you go to the emergency room it costs a fortune. If you buy certain drugs it costs a fortune. Go to Walmart and buy generic drugs where it doesn't get charged against our insurance company. Go and get your physical so we know you're well.

Self-Learning System

An adaptive, self-learning organization is a lot less stressful for the CEO. For that to happen people have to know they're in charge of decisions within their area of responsibility.

BUTCH: At one time, I had a lot of decisions to make. Problems would escalate. They'd find their way to me. As our Five Hundred Leaders initiative took hold, decision-escalation to me became almost non-existent. The system was learning from itself and problems were being resolved as they arose.

Previously people would call me on a regular basis wanting my help. I would get calls about hiring and firing people, but that's gone away. HR takes care of that. They can make decisions. They have a budget. Those are not my decisions to make.

Because of my engineering skills there were lots of things that came to me. Technical problems get resolved elsewhere. Life gets better for the CEO when other people are capable of *collective creativity* which is what we have more to talk about in the next chapter.

Insights

AT's leadership team members began to recognize a sense of unity within the entire organization and across processes. The PCO created value for associates. They want to be here and wanted others to join. Associates were referring family and friends:

> *I had a friend who was married to an employee of Abrasive Technology. I read about the company on the Internet. I saw words like "process centered" and "self-manage." That immediately got my attention. After years of working in an environment with so many layers of management, I couldn't understand how a company can excel when I couldn't find one manager in the org chart. I applied to Abrasive Technology, and the rest is history. I'm excited and challenged every day to do and to think. That's so refreshing.*

> *—AT Associate*

Associates were participating. They were sticking their necks out—making decisions, asking questions, offering suggestions. Greater freedom and flexibility allowed for a better balance between work and life. The company had transitioned from a limited focus on plant, capital, machinery, and metrics to an integrated holistic worldview. And at its heart is the human being.

Heartbeat

- Experiment and see what happens.
- Tolerate not knowing.
- Know the why.
- Communicate, communicate, communicate.
- Language matters.
- Lower stress, boost productivity.
- Care.

Chapter Five

Collective Creativity

Maybe you can remember your first day of school, the first day on the job, the first time you had to handle a new problem. There is always a first time. New situations are challenging, but they're opportunities to adapt, to behave differently, to try something new, to gain experience and grow. You had to think on your feet. You had to make decisions. You had to communicate. Novel problems confront each of us every day. To do something you've never done before is an act of creativity.

You can't measure creativity. You can measure the results of it. You can copy results. But you can't copy creativity itself because creativity emerges from engaged individuals, a safe and trusting culture, and a supportive organizational structure that promotes teaching, learning, and communication.

The Curious Mind

The creative mind is curious. It likes to be free to ask questions:

- What is this?
- Why are we doing it?

- How can we do it better?
- Do we need to do it in the first place?
- What are we missing?
- What else can we use this for?
- What happens if we do it another way?
- What happens if we make a modification?
- How can we see this differently?
- Do we understand the current situation correctly?
- What are alternative perspectives?
- What would be a better question?
- What are we learning here?

In a June 2006 TED talk, educational guru Sir Ken Robinson said that creativity is as important in the 21st century as literacy was in the 19th. Widespread literacy helped catapult industry forward. Today, creative collaboration is the springboard to higher states of organizational intelligence and function.

Creativity is human potential in action. It's the ability to be imaginative and inventive, to see and act in original ways. Creativity is sometimes thought of as an isolated individual act, something belonging to a genius; a special gift. But creativity is in all of us.

Robinson is passionate about encouraging children's creativity, but current school systems are not listening. They are doing the opposite with teaching to the test. Curiosity and creativity are natural human impulses. Experimenting is trying something new and seeing what can be learned.

Creative Structures

Traditional manufacturing companies organize around product lines. The product line has a product manager, a sales person, a customer service person, an administrative person, and a manufacturing person. The product line has a research and development group. Then the same structure repeats for another product line right beside it. Each of these product lines may not know what the others are doing and have their own set of rules, methodologies and management styles. They are silos.

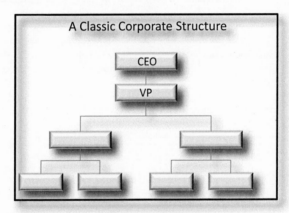

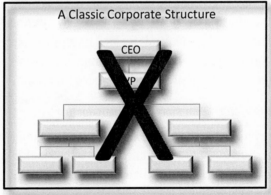

Figure 5: The Classic, Siloed Organization

By contrast, in a *process-centered organization* (PCO), customer service is the process responsible for all products of the company from a customer service perspective. Similarly, manufacturing is a process; finance is a process, and so on.

Coach	Center of Excellence	Process	Process Engineer
		Associate Development and Resources	
		Compliance	
	Administration	Finance	
		Information Technology	
		MRP	
		Quality Assurance	
		Machining	
	Production	Assembly	
		Finishing	
	Customer Communication	Marketing	
		Sales	
		Customer Service	
	Engineering	Research, Development & Engineering	
		Product Engineering	
	Leadership	Business Strategy	
		Business	

Figure 6: The Process-Centered Organization

PCO fosters collective creativity because it encourages teams to make their own decisions. Earlier, we defined a process as a collection of sequential tasks. Examples are customer service, finance, assembly, or machining. Teams are organized by process and led by a process engineer and coach.

A process engineer's responsibilities are to:

- Define and monitor process metrics for throughput, productivity, cost, and quality that balance the needs of associates, company, and customers
- Teach and coach team members on the process

- Assess, monitor, and evaluate performance on process tasks along with the coach according to the Individual Associate Development Plans (IADP) process.
- Continue to analyze and communicate the current and future needs of the process
- Work with other process engineers and teams to align processes, resources and capital with the goals of business strategy
- Understand the PCO and be able to facilitate learning of the cultural system to all associates
- Develop actions to meet annual business roadmap and goals

A coach's responsibilities are to:

- Know, understand, support and assist the implementation of short- and long-term business strategies for associates
- Document problems and support resolutions of conflicts
- Hire, assign, and separate associates as process teams require
- Coach, counsel, support, build relationships, inspire, educate, provide training, mentor, and discipline with input from process engineer
- Work with process engineers and associates to develop and monitor the IADP in conjunction with business strategy and process goals as defined by the IADP process
- Continually work to support and improve understanding of human resources guidelines and compliance
- Understand the PCO and be able to facilitate learning of the cultural system to all associates

- Develop actions to meet annual business roadmap and goals

Part of a coach's job is to understand the company's current and future projections, and then make necessary adaptations. If the company is going to grow at 20 percent a year in a specific area, which people will be needed? If there is a planned expansion in the assembly process, the coach will put together a plan to get the right people in the right place, with the right skill set.

Coaches assist with individual associate development while holding three perspectives—the company, the associate, and the customer. Coaches work with associates to help improve: from both process and personal perspectives.

An order-fulfillment team member is often hired with skills in one subprocess, such as machining, assembly, or finishing. As an associate learns other process skills, they can become a member of more teams, enabling their rapid move to where the work is. As team members learn more tasks they understand more about how their process fits in the whole organization. Because of this wide experience, associates have a more realistic understanding of challenges, limits, and capabilities of what can (and can't) be done. With a broader perspective, teams become better equipped to make their own decisions.

Associates have ongoing support for workplace self-development. Centers of excellence are resources to teams providing leadership, individual development, best practices, training, and support.

Let's use the center of excellence for a customer communications associate as an example. Does a customer service associate properly answer the phone? What's the protocol for answering the phone? Does everyone answer same way? Is this an opportunity to teach and learn? Does the associate need to learn how to negotiate? If yes, a coach will recommend a negotiation class. Once a process is defined, the coach's responsibility is to ensure qualified associates are available to perform the tasks of the process. Even so, there is overlap. Coaches can help design systems and process engineers coach on occasion.

For personal development, Myers-Briggs Type Inventory (MBTI) helps associates learn their own communication preferences. Using other developmental tools, they improve their interactions with people, including the ability to work together more effectively as a team, as well as improved communications with family, friends, and communities outside work.

Many Minds

In his 2011 book, *Thinking, Fast and Slow*, Daniel Kahneman writes that organizations are better at making decisions than individuals are. You can be deluded by judging a decision by its result instead of how the decision was made.

The outcome of any decision is subject to the process, as well as many factors, some of them unknown, even luck. It's possible to make a bad decision and still come out OK—once in a blue moon. But a team's collective intelligence is more likely to avoid blind spots because the group will tend to behave within norms that modify extremes or impulsive decision making.

At AT, teams are trained to make many decisions without input from their process engineers. When decisions are arrived at through peer interaction they are more meaningful. If you don't communicate effectively, you end up with only one perspective—your own.

James Surowiecki's *Wisdom of the Crowd* shows how groups of individuals estimate general knowledge better than a single expert. Collective decision making minimizes biases. Groups tend to curb excesses. There are more voices and data points. This is a compelling reason to include different perspectives.

An even more compelling reason for teams to operate as self-organizing systems is the confidence-boosting emotional connection. When people have a voice and feel heard, their contribution is no longer an abstraction. It's more tangible when teams decide what to do as a collective unit.

BUTCH: Delivery and requests for expedited delivery is a very common issue for every manufacturer, as it is for AT. It usually starts with a customer request for immediate shipment of a part. In the past, we made it faster just because the customer asked us, even though it would disrupt our flow process and make more parts late. To improve our on-time delivery, customer service started to ask questions about the need for delivery and saw that just a few customers made up the majority of the requests. They noticed these same customers that "needed" faster delivery also asked for shipments to be sent the cheapest and slowest way. It didn't make sense. Did the customer really need it faster? When we added a charge for faster delivery, we quickly learned many did not need faster delivery—it was just their standard operating procedure.

We also discovered customers were "shopping" us for better delivery by calling sales, manufacturing, engineering, or anyone who would "help" them with delivery. The situation was getting fouled up because everyone wanted to help meet the customer's needs and gave them answers from their own perspectives. No answers were the same. As a result, the customer was confused and manufacturing didn't know how to proceed.

There were customers who had a need for delivery and were willing to pay, but we couldn't do it. When we started our process-centered organization, customer service became AT's voice for all orders in the system. The customer service process team was responsible for getting the information needed and responding to customers with what we could do while balancing the needs of our customers, associates, and the company. Most of the time, we were able to meet their needs. There were, however, times customer service would have to tell a customer we could not deliver faster. When this happened, customers would complain to customer service and ask for their boss or someone else in the company. Customer service was responsible for the customer communication, so there was nowhere to go. Then they'd call me, or they'd call the process engineer of manufacturing or sales. They might call 10 people.

I knew most of the customers. Bob would call me and say, "Hey, Butch, Buddy. How are you? How's your golf? And, by the way, I have a major problem. Mary in customer service isn't helping me. We need this product yesterday and she is charging me an expedite fee. You need to do something about it."

My response could have been, "OK. I'll get on it. I'll call and find out what's up." This would have stuck me in the middle of every customer issue, and customer service would no longer have the customer's confidence. Instead, I decided not to do this. I'd say, "I don't know why we are unable to meet your request." So I'd call Mary and we'd have all three of us on the line.

I'd ask, "Mary, what did you tell Bob about delivery?" She would say something like we couldn't do it in two weeks, give her reasons, what could be done, and at what cost.

Then I'd say, "Thanks, Mary. Bob, that's your answer. This is all we can do." It made a difference to Mary to be supported in this way.

Over the next three to six months, I received fewer and fewer calls. Customers would call somebody else—the head of manufacturing or head of sales. I reminded each of them: "You cannot accept the call. You may say, "Thank you for the call and I will send you to Mary. She knows the answer."

TANYA: In the beginning, this was a learning process for members of the Leadership Team and especially for our Sales Process Team Members. Naturally, they wanted to help. But it wasn't helping. It was hurting. It caused confusion and information wasn't getting into the system. That meant we couldn't meet customers' need or track what was happening. Change was hard.

But when people started to understand the flow of the organization, they got it. It really worked, and it made customer service feel a lot better about their jobs. Customer service was recording customer interactions in the system, so there was a good history for anyone to review. Customers no longer received conflicting reports from different areas of the company and had a credible source of information about their orders.

If a team is normally spending $2,000 and it suddenly jumps [to] $20,000, it's the process engineer's responsibility to ask why [the] change occurred. It may be justifiable or maybe people [did]n't understand what they're supposed to be doing. It could [als]o be that the company didn't do an adequate job of training, [co]mmunicating, or educating. Or a team didn't understand [wh]at's reasonable…a perfect opportunity for learning. In most [co]mpanies, if you spend one nickel over what's expected, you're [in] big trouble. But this is not the AT way.

No one can foresee everything. If there's a disaster, the [co]mpany is going to have to adapt. If a machine breaks down, [we] have to fix it, even if it wasn't planned or in the budget. We [dea]l with the unexpected. We're going to buy whatever we need. [Ini]tially, this perspective drove people crazy. They had been so [foc]used on the rules we'd thrown away.

[Bu]siness Roadmap

BUTCH: Rather than the traditional way of creating a [ve]ry rigid budget where executives demand unrealistic budget [tig]htening and middle managers pad their needs to compensate., [AT]'s process develops a more flexible, direction-setting business [roa]dmap. The roadmap is broader than a budget, as it includes [exp]ected financials, human resource requirements, focus [pro]ducts and markets, capital expenditures, goals, and global [eco]nomic forecasts. It is a one-year roadmap where each process [tea]m gets together to talk about what they need and why, and [ma]kes suggestions for what they plan to do. It's important not to [cre]an expectation that all proposed ideas will happen. That's the [mo]st difficult thing. It has to be clear this is input for the broader [pic]ture.

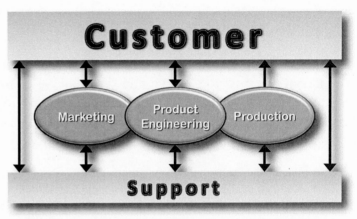

Figure 7: Business process and communications flow

BUTCH: There are always exceptions that require further review. Let's stay with the customer service example where Mary had to tell the customer we couldn't do what they asked. After receiving more information, she realized the situation was more critical than she had thought and would require information from many processes to meet their need.

For example, let's say this key customer wants faster delivery yet we can't do what the customer wants unless we make significant changes everywhere which would affect our costs, our associates, several processes and our product flow.

Mary decides to ask the business process engineer and the people the changes would affect to get involved and rethink the decision. Together, they analyze the situation and determine what's possible and what's not. It is amazing what associates are willing to do when they understand the bigger picture!

Now the decision becomes a balancing act between disruptive change and satisfying this customer right now. What are the consequences of change? Can we really do what the customer is asking? If the answer is yes, we all agree to make necessary changes.

Mary then calls the customer and says, "We understand how important this is to you. We've said "no," but we've taken a second look and we're trying to accommodate you. We're not going to be able to make one-week delivery, but we can make it in 10 days."

Mary is now the hero.

This fundamental change in how we looked at processes changed how customer service associates felt about their jobs. It changed how the customer responds to what our customer services associates are doing. When teams make their own decisions it builds trust for everyone, including the customer. The process becomes more efficient for the customer, the company, and the associates. It's a win-win-win. Many minds can accomplish so much more than one.

Deciding Together

To demonstrate trust in associates and help them learn about budgeting, teamwork, goal-setting, and decision-making, we initiated a program where each process team received $2,000 to spend in whatever way they thought would best facilitate their work. In the past, we had often received complaints from associates who didn't have what they needed to do their jobs. These complaints were often about not having the right screwdriver, a chuck, or a set of gauges. They were relatively small dollar purchases, but caused them great irritation. So we gave them an allotment of $2,000 (it eventually increased to $3,000) and asked them to decide what was important.

Here's how it worked: The process engineer w together with each process team to explain what th program was about. Each team member was tasked t list of what they wanted, along with the approximate p had one week to think about it and return their reque process engineer, who then compiled them into one l she also asked each associate to prioritize the complet total $2,000, not a penny more. Then the process eng with the groups to discuss and make final choices o buy. Everyone learned how difficult it was to decide spend limited funds.

This process continued for several years. The smaller and smaller. The complaints stopped. Peop trusting that they really could get what they needed t work.

As a result of lessons learned from the $2,000 we then opened up the purchasing process. All asso process teams could purchase what they needed, needed it, without approval signatures required (e capital equipment purchases). Process engineers c spend more time looking at the overall cost drivers— purchases—of their process.

This is another example of clearly defining and processes to remove real or perceived obstacles.

What matters is how the decisions are made. We in most people's behavior, and for the exceptions system in place.

From a process perspective, a process engineer kr his team normally spends. Each month, he gets a lis and services the process has purchased, with associat

First, the business strategy team gives everyone in the company an idea of where the business is currently, products and markets to focus on, an economic perspective and major initiatives for the coming year. The question is always: How can we do better than we did last year?

Group members offer ideas, needs, and wants, so suggestions can be compared with input from other groups and seen in the broader context. What matters is what's best for the company. Then we ask groups to prioritize based on available resources and the needs of the company for the next year.

TANYA: The business road map process is amazing. It includes more than just numbers. It's an opportunity for everyone in the company to have a voice, whether it is a suggestion, an idea, an improvement, a project, a piece of equipment, or a training course. It's collective creativity and reaches out to every person in every process across the entire company.

Each process team, including the process engineer, sort and prioritize their list of ideas. These ideas are presented at the global leadership meeting to discuss and prioritize from a company-wide perspective. After making a financial review of the resulting budget containing the prioritized items, the roadmap is approved by the business strategy team. The loop is then complete. The company takes a collective breath for reflection.

AT benefits from the wisdom of the crowd. In this way, the business is grounded in reality. It is aligned with realistic processes of the whole company. Everything is put together and digested and becomes the new platform for a continually evolving structure: the annual kick-off meeting.

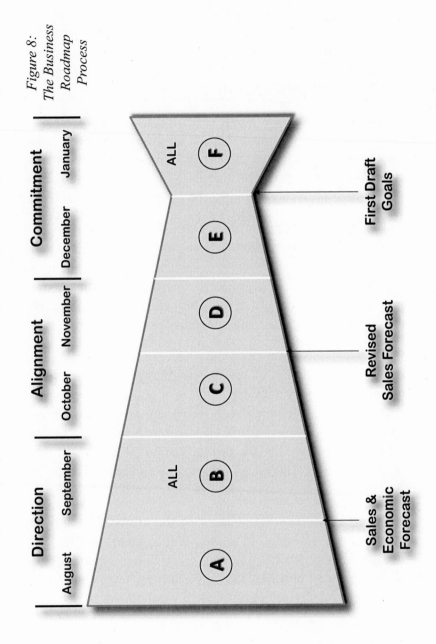

Figure 8:
The Business
Roadmap
Process

A. Business Strategy Meeting
1. Short Term Direction
2. Long Term Vision

B. All Process Teams Meetings
1. Ideas for Process Improvements
2. What does it take: People, Projects & Capital Expenditures?
3. Expected results

C. Global Leadership Meeting
1. Global Economic Forecast Review
2. Presentations from Process Team Meeting
3. Connect Time

D. Business Strategy Meeting
From a company-wide, global and long-term perspective, evaluate the financial impact of the input from the roadmap process, ensure alignment with long-term vision and agree on the extent to which the company can fund the requested:
1. Capital Expenditures & Significant Discretionary Spending
2. Proposed Goals
3. Proposed Projects
4. Manpower Additions

E. Business Strategy & Leadership Team Meeting
Discuss and agree upon the final Roadmap

F. January Kick-Off Meetings (All Associates/All Locations)
Present Roadmap Summary

Final Business Roadmap Includes:
1. Assumptions
2. Economic Perspective
3. Focus, Products & Markets
4. Capital Expenditures, Projects & Discretionary Spending
5. Manpower required
6. Financials by Process
7. Cash Forecast
8. Goals by Process

Everyone Welcome

TANYA: The annual kick-off meeting is held at each of AT's global sites. Butch shares a summary of the business roadmap results. This is where everyone learns about what the company is doing, what it's planning to do, and where the challenges are. He shares plans by process for sales, people, equipment, and facilities. Associates learn what's happening in diverse areas of the company-products and sales, acquisitions, learning and development initiatives, and financial results.

You encourage cooperation through the structure of your organization. Recapping the year reminds everyone of accomplishments they tend to forget. The entire company is lifted up by the collective effort, and the remembering together creates emotional bonds for us as a company. Being part of the group and knowing what's going on gives people a sense of group purpose, a sense of belonging. That is aided by how the company is organized. People need to see how they positively impact the organization.

BUTCH: The kick-off meeting is organized into mini-reports: what happened in the past year, profit sharing bonus announcement, what's happening in the world, and what's happening next year. We reflect on the year that just passed and look at where we are now.

As an example, in one meeting I forecasted that the economy would be down slightly, but we were financially sound and would be ok. I reminded them that we all got a raise the previous year. We increased incentive compensation. We increased profit-sharing. All of us had some new opportunity. We continued to invest in capital equipment and built a new facility. The company made more money than the previous year and increased sales. The company won, you won, we all won, the community won.

And then I asked, "Were last year's results better than you had thought?"

No one remembers everything we did. The idea behind reminding them of the many things we accomplished is to blow their socks off. And it does.

When we present the holistic view of the company, new associates are surprised. They never had anyone tell them about what was going on in so much detail. This leads to greater understanding and becomes the new norm of seeing the big picture and everyone's place in it. The whole organization moves to a new level.

For new Manufacturing with Heart clients, we try to shift their perspective from tactical, fixing problems to a more holistic view. The problem-solution mindset will only take you so far. Real change comes from an effort to develop everyone.

No matter how well you do, there will always be room for improvement. The question is how can you develop people to higher levels of function and satisfaction even more than they are today? How can process improve? How can the collaborative environment improve? How can happiness grow? Perfection may be unattainable, but we'd like to get a lot closer to the vision of developing 500 leaders.

Working Laboratory

Offshoring manufacturing jobs may lower costs in the short term, but it does long-term damage. That's because it's not just tasks that are exported, but know-how and innovation. Countries like India and China are making large investments in research and development infrastructure, which has long-term impact.

According to Robert Atkinson of the Brookings Institution Metropolitan Policy Program, his organization and the Information Technology and Innovation Foundation are lobbying the federal government to invest $500 million to establish 20 "manufacturing universities." However, manufacturers don't have to wait around for them to act.

BUTCH: We learned by doing—which is something anyone can do. As we worked on evolving our culture, we still made and developed new products. Even though we spent a vast amount of time and money on self-development, process, and culture change, it wasn't a full-time job. The business of the company keeps improving as we tweak processes and introduce new initiatives. Everything is in movement. It has to be.

When I made the choice that the company needed to focus on people, we hired the Center of Creative Leadership (CCL) for leadership development, where we had little expertise. At the same time, we wanted to create a unique culture with their guidance. We wanted to have our own experience of designing something from the inside. We chose our own path toward a positive, collaborative environment. We wanted to learn from our mistakes. When people visit our facilities, they notice a difference.

The world has changed considerably over the last 20 years. Today, companies like Manufacturing with Heart have greater insight into how organization, culture, and technology work together.

TANYA: We experimented with apprenticeships to give people an opportunity to do something entirely different. Results varied, but everyone gained new understanding. This created fellowship, loyalty, and mutual respect. As an example, people on the shop floor discovered that those in customer service worked really hard. These weren't the soft, high-paying jobs they had imagined. Some people made successful transitions; others went back to their old jobs with a new appreciation for what they had. People told their stories, and other people learned.

At one time, there were about eight people at different stages of apprentice machining. Some were taking high-level online courses to improve their skills. There were people who wanted to become apprentices but didn't yet have the basic math. Coaches enrolled them in online courses so they could pass the math test. The idea was to support people to try to expand their skills and themselves where AT needed increased capabilities.

The Positive Environment

BUTCH: Creating a positive environment affects people inside and outside of the company. One gesture of kindness, or doing the right thing, is often repeated. Just paying our bills on time touches the outside community. Accounts payable's job is to pay bills on time, not to figure out how not to pay them. I don't care if it's the mailman or if it's the guy from the janitorial service who sweeps the floors. They tell me they love being at AT because they're treated with respect.

All the people from our accounting firm want to come to our audit because we're prepared. We are nice to them, we are calm, and we are professional. FedEx likes coming to our place because we're technologically advanced. We can lock into their systems the way they want so they don't have a lot of issues with what we do.

Customers get consistent information about our capabilities to fill their needs. This gives them a sense of trust.

TANYA: Inside the company, we can tell when people are happy. When people at work are enjoying themselves the conversation is light. They smile more. It's banter about everyday life and what people are looking forward to doing. People are more present. You can tell when the opposite is true—when conversations take the form of demands and finger-pointing: "You need to do this; you didn't get that done."

BUTCH: Some people are looking for happiness and work at being happy. Others tend to find all the bad stuff and concentrate on the negative. You see it in the perspective they have. Here's a story I like:

An old man is walking from one city to the next. On the road between the two cities he meets a young fellow walking in the opposite direction.

The young man asks, "How friendly are the people where you've come from?"

The old man responds, "How friendly are people where you're coming from?"

The young man answers, "They're not very nice people."

The old man says, "That's what you'll find where you're going, too."

TANYA: Perspective is something we carry around with us. Many times, people don't know how their behavior is affecting themselves or the people around them. This is one of the reasons that all new hires take the MBTI class, and other self-development tools.

We chose to certify associates to administer MBTI to bring that competency into the company. We would wait until we had 10 to 12 new people and then have an MBTI class for them as a group. It's such a profound experience. After class, associates return to their teams and talk to others about it. People remember their own experience with MBTI and their own preferences for communication. It becomes a lively topic of conversation and keeps self-awareness alive. It's like a wave of collective learning. HR professionals and coaches are now coming in as new hires with knowledge and understanding of many self-development tools such as MBTI.

BUTCH: Myers-Briggs and EQ Certifications can be obtained in a relatively short time. However, where the expertise required is deep we've gone outside. We used Susanne Cook-Greuter and CCL to train the trainers.

Any business owner or CEO has to have a high level of interest in his own personal development experience. It is an absolute prerequisite for transforming to a holistic company.

An example of collective creativity came about with communities of practice.

Communities of Practice

Anyone can suggest a new initiative. Some are generated by leadership. A cross-disciplinary group can come together to try something out, put in place a pre-process test-bed, create a prototype, solve a problem, a place to explore a thought, or address a need. We called our groups *Communities of Practice* (CoP).

TANYA: We started a Green CoP which eventually turned into a permanent process we call Sustainability that resulted in meaningful savings for the company and for the environment.

CoPs are usually short-term. One such CoP was tasked with creating a learning center. The group decided how to go about it and then made it happen. They did it by working together. When it was finished, they moved on. The group dissolved.

Associates enjoy CoPs. It's a learning experience; a chance to grow and change. It doesn't involve taking on permanent responsibilities like their regular jobs. Associates experience leading. They learn to collaborate by sharing leadership on various parts of a project. They do something different. They get to meet different people.

BUTCH: There's value to bringing people together from different processes. There might be somebody from the machine shop, somebody from finance, and somebody from IT. It's not your friends or the same work group. When people start understanding we are all the same it helps to dissolve we-them boundaries.

We noticed that people unfamiliar with the group topic can ask naïve questions. This is a good thing because sometimes these questions lead to new insights. People with more knowledge would never stop to ask themselves such basic questions. It helps break new ground. The group learns from itself.

CoP members discover that associates in other teams are really kind of nice people. They have good ideas and they have kids and families. They aren't so different. They like to go to dinner and they have similar interests. CoPs generate conversations between people that wouldn't happen otherwise. Then people go back to their departments and talk about it. New feelings spread throughout the company. It opens people's minds and hearts and builds community

TANYA: This shows up in spontaneous acts of kindness. People get to know each other. If anybody gets hurt, gets in trouble, they help each other so much with their families and personal challenges.

If somebody's in the hospital or sick, people will visit every day. Several people have had cancer. Associates collected donations. They took food to them—almost every day—not for just a week, but for months, or even a year. They pick them up, take them to the doctor. They just care for them. The community pulls together. We didn't ask them to do that, but we're so grateful it happens. They created a community of care by themselves.

Appreciation

TANYA: Earlier, we discussed ritual and how celebration binds groups together. AT holds annual appreciation dinners where everyone with over 5 years of service is invited. It deepens the collective experience. People enjoy themselves and share their stories and experiences.

For me, what has even more impact on associates is our annual kick-off meeting. This is a place where gratitude and enjoyment comes out big time, collective understanding grows, and clarity about how much everyone accomplished. People feel comfortable, safe, excited and energized by knowing and understanding the big picture. Everyone feels connected.

On that day, nobody walks out of the meeting who doesn't feel that same way. This is done exactly the same at every site around the world. Everyone gets the same message. It's so important. It's genuine feeling.

BUTCH: When it comes to appreciation, I don't like Recognition Programs because they feel insincere. I prefer just walking around and making heart-felt positive comments and singing happy birthday on someone's birthday or sending an email to give specific comments about a success. It feels right.

There is a difficulty with public recognition awards and I learned this the hard way. Many years ago, an associate designed and manufactured a new fixture on her own time. It saved the company a lot of money. It was really effective.

I made a big deal out of it and gave her $500 in front of everybody. She and her husband designed it at home and brought it in to work. They had no expectation of reward because we didn't have such a program. So I gave them an award in front of lots of people who were now using their cool invention.

Then the problems started. Other people claimed the inventor had asked them questions about her fixture. They felt it was their idea as well. They felt entitled to a reward. It turned really ugly. Now it is part of an associate's tasks to improve the process however they can. The monetary rewards are increased incentive compensation and profit sharing.

TANYA: What does work, however, is looking into someone's eyes and saying, "You did a good job" on this or that. Being specific is important. Just ask about what someone's doing or how they are, and then really listen to and acknowledge them for their achievements.

Consistency and sincerity matter. If you do it every day, it works. But you shouldn't do it only because it's on your to-do list. People realize their turn for being appreciated is going to come. What you say, however, must be sincere. It can't be forced.

Recognition Programs in general are superficial. They take time and effort to administer. A more effective use of resources is to develop individuals and the leadership teams in a general framework for authentic and transparent interactions. People have said to me many times that they feel the sincerity when I look into their eyes and say, "I appreciate what you've done." Encouragement and recognition come from the heart.

Heartbeat

- Creative minds are curious.
- Corporate structures either prevent or encourage collective creativity.
- Higher individual levels of development make for better group interactions.
- How decisions are made are more important than outcomes.
- Groups are more likely to make accurate predictions than individuals.
- Active group participation makes people feel included.
- A working laboratory is a place to try something different.
- Genuine recognition makes a positive difference.
- Communities of Practice are short-term groups bringing together people from different processes for a specific purpose.
- Sincere appreciation creates a sense of belonging.
- Apprentice Programs encourage people to try new jobs and gives them a new and realistic appreciation of their current roles, other roles, people and groups.
- Communities of care emerge from a positive and productive environment.
- Creativity is in all of us.

Chapter Six

Trust

The best way to find out if you can trust somebody is to trust them.

— *Ernest Hemingway*

Survey after survey shows most industry leaders consistently fail to execute on strategy. For a long time, leaders have understood what they should do—create structures for collective creativity, treat people with respect and dignity, and give them the support they need. But they find this easier said than done. What's the problem?

Trust

All relationships are based on trust. For more than 2,000 years, the Analects has influenced leaders. One of its main principles is cultivation of trustworthiness. Business author Stephen R. Covey calls trust the glue of life. If leadership doesn't genuinely believe people can be trusted, then no matter how many change initiatives they try, they are doomed to fail. Command

and control remains the status quo. Rules and surveillance sucks time and energy that could be put to better use.

So what are we talking about when we say trust?

Five Perspectives

1. Trust is openness, letting go of control. For that to happen, you need courage to risk being vulnerable—and responsible for the outcome. For a leader, there is no freedom without responsibility. With greater trust comes more safety for people to open up.

2. Care fosters trust. Initially people are concerned they may be harmed, so at first they are naturally defensive. A safe environment encourages trust.

3. Trust is your belief in competency. You trust that people have aptitude to do what they need to do.

4. Trust is reliability. Are you consistent in your actions? Do words match deeds? We call this DWYSYWD (Do What You Say You Will Do).

5. Trust is sincere intention. When you say what you mean and mean what you say, you are sincere. This shows you're to be trusted. If you have a hidden agenda, people read right through it. People can feel if you're open, sincere, reliable, competent, and caring.

As associates trust they won't be punished for taking reasonable risks, two different kinds of benefits arise. First, trying something becomes less scary. Curiosity, that driver of innovation, takes the lead. An atmosphere of interest, engagement, and often fun grows. Second, learning expands exponentially as minds are freed up to explore. Learning ripples out in all directions.

BUTCH: A palpable sense of relief spreads through the workplace. It's so simple. We're all trying to do our best. Mistakes happen. We're human. Just do what we can to learn from errors and go on. "Do the right thing" became one of our slogans. Some say that the right thing for one person might not be the right thing for another. That's true, but over time, most folks come to a deeper meaning: If you're doing something and it doesn't feel right in your belly, stop. Ask questions. Try to get to the "why" of what you're feeling and trust your instincts.

This creates an amazing atmosphere. The troubles and problems in business come and go, but with this philosophy and hard work, a company can persevere and continue to provide good jobs for employees and their families.

Stamina

BUTCH: Change causes some pain. If you're going to create a culture of trust, you need stamina, money, and patience. You need to be clear on what you're doing and where you're going. How much of each of these you need depends on how big a risk you are taking.

TANYA: You need to have realistic expectations. Transformational change based on a process-centered organization will be disruptive. You need to go into this change process with your eyes open. If you, as CEO or business owner, get cold feet, then all bets are off. You need to trust yourself and have a firm commitment to stay the course. You can expect that things will get worse before they get better.

This is really no different from any investment. In general, you first have to allocate resources—before you see any benefit. The curve on the graph will go down before it goes up. Then, it's likely to go up a lot. Expect resistance at first.

BUTCH: When we put in the PCO, even the three or four people who were closest to me had concern about how well it was going to work.

TANYA: Even I felt that. There were times I wanted Butch to go back, but he stayed the course. Unless someone's willing to suffer the short-term pain, change will fail. We're biologically hardwired to want immediate rewards. The mature adult learns to delay gratification, so this is back to the ancient idea of leadership as a practice.

BUTCH: The movement is from transactional to transformational. Transactional is where you measure everything. You put in rules and regulations. This is the opposite of trust. It's attempting to control based on what's happened in the past. The focus is on the short-term fix. A large public company can't afford the necessary dip before the upside. Investors in public companies demand short-term results. Transactional measures only kick the can further down the road.

Default Power

A trusted person assumes a level of control for making independent decisions. There can be no autonomy without trust. Trust is a two-way street. If I trust you, you're likely to trust me. If I distrust you, then you certainly won't trust me. So what is the default? Trust or distrust? This is an important point.

Nudge: Improving Decisions About Health, Wealth, and Happiness by Richard Thaler and Cass Sunstein, is a book about behavioral economics and the power of default positions.

One of their examples is a 401(k) retirement plan. Instead of trying to coerce people to save for retirement with an active choice to put aside a portion of their paycheck, a more effective way is to set up the default structure to opt in. This in no way limits freedom of employees. They can opt out at any time. But they need to make an active choice to do so. This way they are more likely to think about the consequences of robbing future Peter to pay present-day Paul.

Studies have shown how all of us are notoriously bad about predicting the future. This is why so few Americans and others save enough to retire. Environment encourages behavior. So what kind of behavior do you want to encourage? A trusting culture looks different from a distrusting one.

If you've visited your local DMV or other government agency lately, you've probably noticed signs listing all the things you can't do. This is a culture of "No." It may seem cheaper to put up signs and invent rules than put time and effort into encouraging people to develop. But it's short-term thinking.

It's easy to understand why people are distrustful. You see a disconnection between promise and action all the time. Political campaign promises are broken. Infrastructure projects are late. Companies euphemistically "restate their earnings." Budgets are revised upward again and again in the light of new contingencies. All of this doesn't necessarily mean people are willfully lying. The world is ever changing and more complex than you can imagine. Even with the latest technological resources you can't foresee everything. You have to continually adapt to new realities.

According to a 2014 *IndustryWeek* article, a recent Gallup survey found that companies with the most engaged work teams "have significantly higher productivity, profitability, and customer ratings, less turnover and absenteeism, and fewer safety incidents than those in the bottom 25 percent."[1]

1   *IndustryWeek*, November, 2014 p.8 Patricia Panchak, Editor-in-Chief

Building a culture of trust won't happen overnight. But step-by-step, long-term developmental effort pays off, as it has for companies in other sectors; Whole Foods, Trader Joe's, Starbucks, and many other people-driven companies. Trust allows for far more effective systems. When people learn they are trusted, good things happen. Yet, we're not being naïve. Trust has its boundaries.

Boundaries

TANYA: For us everyone is trustworthy until proven otherwise. Violation of trust is a boundary issue. When this happens we discuss it. We want to find out where the boundary was and what's going on. Repairing broken trust is not always possible. But it could be a simple lack of communication, or a misunderstanding. Often, those can be easily fixed.

BUTCH: But if it's deep-seated, such as a person will never be competent, or someone is out to do harm, then there is no way we can repair that kind of broken trust.

As for the problem of competency, the idea is to fix the bad and improve the good. You need to address both of these. It helps generate trust by honestly talking about the situation. People know when there's a problem. If it isn't addressed it will fester. If you don't bring it out into the open then they'll wonder what else you're hiding. These can be difficult conversations, but they're necessary. This way there's no hidden agenda, no secrets.

Every team member knows when someone has gone over the edge. Once that happens, getting back in is going to be tough. Team members know what's going on. Groups operate with norms. There are people saying, "That doesn't make sense to me," so teams self-regulate.

Early in our leadership development, CCL facilitated an off-site leadership meeting for about 40 of our managers, supervisors and coordinators. I wanted to attend and learn, but also I didn't want to get in the way of group process. I decided to sit the meeting out and attend the final dinner.

This is where I learned an important lesson about boundaries.

On their return, we had a debrief meeting about their learnings. Several attendees announced that they now understood that they could run the company without me or my staff and didn't need us. It felt like a mutiny. We were in shock. A big boundary had been crossed! Despite good intentions for leadership development, what we got wasn't collaborative teamwork but a power grab. We listened to other attendees about their take-aways, called an end to the meeting and scheduled another meeting for the next day. We let them know we appreciated their perspective and wanted them to have more autonomy but they did not yet have the strategic capabilities to run the company.

I always attended leadership meetings after that. Collaboration is a developmental process. Team members have to be ready. Trust takes time and attention.

TANYA: Team members have clear boundaries around expectations of behavior, responsibilities, and required tasks. For example, there's flexibility around attendance, but the expectations are there. When people go too far they're called on it by their peers or their coach or their process engineer.

Trust and Transparency

TANYA: Openness is the antidote to the rumor mill. Rumors breed in an atmosphere of secrecy. Transparency communicates respect. Every time so-called secrets come up it's important to respond. When you're acting for the benefit of the company and associates, very little needs to be confidential. Everything is open to scrutiny. This demonstrates trust.

BUTCH: You have to build trust first. You do this so you can gain consensus around where you're going, what you're doing, and why you're doing it. Gain collective understanding so even if things go down, they will build back up again. If you don't do this groundwork, you'll have constant resistance. You have to avoid the corrosive effect of passive-aggressive behavior. Passive aggression is the only option in a culture that won't allow enough freedom for voices to be heard. You have to listen to dissenting voices and show you heard.

TANYA: We got feedback we weren't listening. We asked a few questions and found out that not listening was in fact, "You're not doing what I want" or "There was no response to my question" or they hadn't heard the response even though something had been done.

BUTCH: One afternoon, I was walking down the hall. An associate came up to me and said, "Hey, Butch, the air conditioner doesn't work." This was not top of my list to worry about that day. I had other things on my mind. I forgot about it, so it didn't get fixed. The view was that I didn't listen.

So we agreed we weren't effectively responding. We asked everyone in the corporation, "What haven't we been listening to?" I asked them to give me a list of things they thought should happen that weren't happening, whatever they were. I wanted at least two from every individual. We ended up with about 300 suggestions. We put all the suggestions up on a big board in the lunchroom so everyone could see them.

We promised we would respond to every one of them, and we did.

Some said, "We need a dollar pay increase."

I said, "No." At least they had an answer.

We listened and answered, and we went through the entire list.

At meetings, I would say, "Look, don't tell me in the hallway that you want something on the list. You have to write it down, confirm it with your name, and we will add it to the list so we both know something is supposed to happen. We'll respond. Until it's on the board it is not for discussion."

We needed to demonstrate we were listening and responding appropriately. We'd scratch off each item on the lunchroom board as we addressed it: OK, we fixed the air conditioner. We bought wrenches, or whatever the items were. We turned down a number of suggestions, but we had made decisions everyone could see. That helped build trust.

Trust and Time

BUTCH: Gaining trust takes time. Interpersonal communication is easier in smaller groups where people know each other. When I buy a company, I think about how long it will take for the people in this company to trust each other and the new management team. One took a year. Realistic expectations should be anywhere from six months to a year. People tend to be more trusting of those they know. This takes time.

Our track record boosts confidence for people in a newly acquired company. Even if at first they don't understand the holistic manufacturing concept and the transformational direction, it allows them to have confidence because of our past development. They can see how people behave in a culture of trust. They know that when something doesn't work we'll make changes so it does.

Stop Measuring Everything

BUTCH: Trust can replace some metrics. For example, if I see an associate made three parts yesterday, I may ask, "Can you do four today?" It has nothing to do with the pure measurement; it's about looking for possibilities to improve.

Actually specifying a number of parts can be limiting. If you tell a person to make 10 parts, they make 10 parts. But could they have made 14? In a culture of trust you can ask them to make as many parts as they can—providing the order calls for it. Again, we don't just want to make parts for inventory. This has become "Butch's Benchmark": Here's what you did. What else can you do? It's not a metric I've imposed. It's trust-based freedom to do what they can do. This gives people a sense of autonomy.

TANYA: We share many metrics with all associates on the performance of the business and processes. Process engineers use metrics to determine where to improve their process. It could be bottlenecks, overtime, systemic process problems, training needs, or additional resources needed. Coaches use metrics to work with individuals to match and improve their capabilities to fit the needs of the processes. For customers we do satisfaction surveys, measure on-time delivery and days to deliver.

We pay attention to four significant business numbers: The level and direction of cash flow, productivity, profitability, and sales. These tell us whether we're collectively doing well or not. Our measurement for productivity is sales divided by hours worked. There is Butch's Fat Index, which is sales divided by the number of people working. This metric gives you some kind of index of whether you've got too many non-value-added people in the system. These are consistent metrics that help judge how we guide the boat.

BUTCH: We use those, but don't really impose them on others except to ask questions that allow change.

We stopped posting delivery charts. For years, we had monthly delivery charts posted everywhere. We quit doing it because people were micromanaging rather than just doing the work to improve flow for delivery.

At the time we put in place an incentive compensation plan, people didn't have the holistic view of the entire system—from raw materials in to product out the door. Our incentive compensation program is now based on team performance, not individual performance. The bonus as a function of good products out the door and hours worked is closely aligned with productivity.

We trusted associates would like it and get money out of it, which they did. In the beginning, the old mindset still held some people in its grip. They didn't trust the system for some time, so they went in and counted the parts. They were looking for ways to get around the new system. This went on for almost two years.

We shared all the numbers. Word spread through the grapevine that the new system would give them the appropriate bonus for the quarter. Eventually, they saw it was fair and worked. We gained trust.

Support

BUTCH: We taught English to Spanish speakers. We brought in an English teacher. We hired attorneys to help with an amnesty program for Mexican immigrants in Los Angeles, California. The attorneys filed all the paperwork for the people who worked for us, and all but one were approved.

TANYA: We used to require high school diplomas for new associates. We no longer do that because not everyone has had the same opportunities. Instead, we make an agreement that within the first six months of hire they must pass the GED. We help them take classes to prepare, and it's been a great success. It's generated trust, gratitude, and loyalty. These efforts feel right. They're helpful for the people we serve, as well as the business. The people we help don't have a sense of entitlement. What's so encouraging about this program is that young or older, millennials or not, people feel like they have to work for what they get.

Expectations

BUTCH: When Indian leader Mahatma Gandhi said, "You must be the change you wish to see in the world," he was making a distinction between words and actions, saying and doing. We encourage people to develop their integrity toward greater understanding, benevolence, responsibility, capability, intention, and reliability. The expectation is that everyone will be responsive. They'll work together, they'll learn, grow, and take advantage of the things that are now being offered, and use them appropriately.

DWYSYWD is the fastest trust generator.

When we acquired a new corporation we set expectations for new employees about what we were going to do to improve their operation. We upgraded the facilities. We put in new bathrooms and lunchrooms. We installed consistent computer and phone systems. We made sure the right machinery was in place to get the job done. We shared our vision for the company and each associate's part in the journey. If you don't do what you say you'll do, associates won't trust you.

We expect associates to use these things to generate something better for this corporation and the people around them. The job of leadership is to clearly and consistently communicate expectations.

Sincerity

TANYA: In a meeting on process design, Butch gave a presentation on what we'd done with PCO, leadership and culture development. He talked about our real-world experience around trust, sincerity, belief in people and risking vulnerability. This was in contrast to others, who had more academic or theoretical backgrounds. No one else had the type of hands-on experience we had. No one had taken risks to be vulnerable and actually transform their business. The reaction to Butch's presentation was emotional and enthusiastic.

BUTCH: I was sitting beside a guy and talking about our culture, about the importance of paying attention to people. He said, "You're serious, aren't you?" I said "Yes." He said, "I can see it in your eyes." When you're sincere people pick up on it.

You have to be vulnerable. You have to show it. Other people feel this and that's how trust works. If you're not sincere, you may get some response. You'll generate something. That may be fine, but you won't get the payback for yourself or for others that you could've gotten. Don't worry about the consequences. Just go do it.

If you want to transform your business, you have to build trust. First, however, you must trust yourself to commit to venturing into the unknown—whatever the consequences are. If the business is going to go to hell, what's the big deal? You can get it back. Building trust is how to start. It's a negotiation. Trust is a belief in a better future. But that won't happen by itself. You have to do something. Trust in the bigger picture. Trust in the spirit that you're aligning yourself with.

This book is about transformation rather than transaction. We're suggesting perspectives you can take, some things you can do. But they're not so prescriptive that you're guaranteed to get the result we ended up with. You have to use these ideas as a basis to build on.

Ultimately it's all about awareness. And that's what we're going to discuss next.

Heartbeat

- A culture of trust doesn't waste resources on unnecessary surveillance and metrics.
- Actions speak louder than words. DWYSYWD is the fastest way to gain trust.
- Be consistent. Show you're sincere.
- Mistakes are inevitable. Accept consequences of all of your actions. Apologize and make amends when necessary.
- Care is taking into account everyone's interests.
- Trust is demonstrated through openness.
- Transparency is the antidote to the rumor mill.
- Competence isn't just skill and knowledge. It includes the willingness and ability to learn.
- Trust has boundaries. Examine trust violations from all five trust perspectives before taking action.
- First, give people the benefit of doubt.
- We communicate trust through word choice.
- Be realistic. Building trust takes time and stamina.
- Pay attention to your intentions, and those of others.
- A leader cultivates trustworthiness.
- Create an environment where people feel safe.
- Make trust your default position.

Chapter Seven

Heart Culture

Like any organization, especially those choosing the path less traveled, AT has its own set of challenges to be sure. Our challenge is not born out of crisis or ego. Our challenges come from daring greatly. With all of the associates of AT, I choose this journey each day and continue to believe in the pure potential of the human spirit that this organization brings out in all of us.

—Daryl Peterman, CEO, AT

Manufacturing with Heart is an evolutionary process of doing and being. What you do changes you. Developing who you are—and the people in your company—leads to a wider range of choices for action.

Heart creates unity of hard and soft. *Gestalt* psychologist Kurt Koffka wrote that the whole is greater than the sum of its parts. When both hard and soft sides are developed, new connections and positive possibilities emerge.

Manufacturing with Heart is how you take the industrial history of metal and add the people side: culture, trust, learning, and environmental development. It's an integrative model. In the past the two sides have been separate. Heart hasn't been there much. Now it is.

Heart is sincere care and engages humans at a very deep level.

Crazy to Learn

Before joining AT, E.R. had been the first in her family to graduate high school. She had gone straight to college as a 16-year old. Without support or guidance, she didn't recognize the consequences of student loans. She thought it was free money. By the time she was 18, she was deeply in debt. She didn't understand how deeply. She dropped out of college and was working two jobs just to make ends meet.

She was overjoyed that AT's job offer meant more money than both of her previous jobs put together.

E.R.: I had gone crazy in college. When I came here [AT], I started to learn who I am and who I wanted to be. This place started to change my outlook. I gained friendships and asked a lot of questions. I'd never met engineers and people who could build robots. I'd never been to a research lab. I learned about higher education and a tuition reimbursement program.

I listened to what other people had learned, even from their mistakes. With help and guidance from AT, I was taking responsibility for my education. I had been given a really good job, and I could go back to school. People in my neighborhood had made other choices: just to work and have kids. If I hadn't come here I would still be working at a pizza shop or something. I am truly grateful.

I'm always listening. I try to adapt and learn. I met my now best friend and roommate through Situation Behavior Impact (SBI). Communication skills training and customer service training has taught me so much. What the people at AT do with people skills is a big deal. If we can't work together, then we're not going to have much success. The amazing part of working here is the people.

I remember one of the lunches we had with Butch. I could barely go up to him and say "Thank you" without getting all emotional. I want to provide. I want to be a person who is strong for my community. I want to be one of those people who lift up the world.

***

Heart culture is open to new experience. It looks for the best in people and makes a place for them to grow.

Heart Is Patient

From its beginning, PCO has been a work in progress, with vision and direction allowing room for change. Learning, testing, growing, and evolving creates strong emotional connection for people within the company.

Veteran sales associate S.W. describes AT as delivering innovative solutions for process improvement. Through patience, curiosity, and courage to change old habits he came to understand and appreciate the company's new transformational way of being.

S.W.: While trying to understand the process-centered organization, I started looking for examples where this was happening in other businesses. Conceptually I knew it made sense. I believed it could only work well with the right people in the right place. I'm fascinated by the number of organizations now moving in this direction.

The first place I recognized a process-centered organization was in a restaurant. The maître d' seated us at a table and took our drink order. A server brought the drinks. Then a waiter took our food order. Then a server brought our food. The concept of PCO was taking shape in my mind. Each person has a function, but behind the scenes is tremendous communication among processes.

Things are much more complicated in an organization like AT. Some people struggled and couldn't or wouldn't embrace it [PCO]. It was very scary to see technical talent go, but I knew this organization has been highly successful for over 40 years and would make it work. This is the right direction to go in. I do everything I can to support it. I had to break a lot of my old habits, but it's getting easier every day.

I came in with my eyes wide open. My entire career with the company has been a field trip; seeing how things are manufactured and meeting new people. AT has offered me that playground. It's been the right kind of company for me to be able to experience the type of customers I can relate to. It's our job to identify similar thinking customers and develop relationships so both companies can collaborate and succeed.

AT showed me the grass is greener on this side of the fence.

Heart Unifies Opposites

Collaboration doesn't emerge overnight. You have to patiently chip away at old prejudices. When you dissolve barriers between "us" and "them" you can experience a tremendous upwelling of collaboration. The payoff is fewer problems, novel solutions, and remarkable goodwill. Sometimes people show their best when things go wrong.

TANYA: It was late in the year, almost year-end shut down time. Suddenly, we had a huge influx of orders. There were many people out sick. Just about everything that could go wrong was going wrong. We were in trouble—and we knew it. There was a lot of product we had to get out in six weeks' time. Things were a mess.

So we said to everyone, "Guys, here's the situation. We have all these orders and expected shipments, and we don't have enough manpower to make it happen—even if we work twenty-four by seven. How are we going to do this?"

We put together a team of people from different parts of the organization. All we told them was, "Figure it out. Get together. Talk about possibilities. See what you can come up with."

They did.

The team put a schedule on a big board every day showing what we were doing: This is what's going out; here's what we're telling this customer. It went from order entry to finish to shipment. We called their effort "all hands on deck."

BUTCH: We knew the office folks, including leadership team members, could put off some of their work for a while. Maybe salaried people could work a couple extra hours at night. Could some people work on the weekend? People pitched in.

Somebody from finance would say, "I'm here. I've got two hands. What can I do?"

It was like a job jar. At one time we actually had a jar. People would list items on piece of paper that needed doing, things that could be done with only 10 minutes training. For example, the note might request help with packing boxes. If somebody had extra time they would pull out a note, and go find where they were needed.

We eventually had one person coordinating tasks from the job jar. They would balance requests with resources. They'd direct people where to go.

TANYA: This is another example of move to the work. When you have some time, it's boring to sit on your hands and wait for other work to come in. Better to ask, "What can I do? Where can I go?" People learn more, which might attract them to another process. It helps them develop their own skills and opportunities for further growth.

We looked for what we could teach the office people in just a few minutes. This would allow people who were more technically competent to do the harder work that took six months to learn. There was incredible camaraderie. This felt really good.

The front desk was packaging while they were answering phones. There was a lot of creativity happening all over the place. Everyone in the entire facility was working together. They were absolutely determined to help and make it happen.

People in the shop gained more respect for people in the office.

That new-found respect worked both ways. People in the office brought a fresh perspective because the work was new to them. Some people even developed new ways of making parts. A woman in finance developed a rapid procedure that was previously taking too long. She opened hearts and minds and people started to bring ideas for her to review.

Long before all of this, there was a wall between the plant and the office. It couldn't have happened 10 years earlier. This experience was a direct result of all the work we had done toward PCO and the learning culture. The experience was like pulling down the Berlin Wall. It all started by saying we needed help and asking, what can you do?

This collaborative feeling remains.

Centering

BUTCH: We said earlier how visitors remark on a sense of calm in our manufacturing plants. People are getting on with their jobs. There's a lack of drama and panic. The world really isn't about to end. When people are encouraged rather than judged, it allows them to bring more of their genuine selves into the workplace. Judging is non-productive.

Instead of making automatic verdicts such as, "I don't like that" or "That's not very good," you can ask questions, be curious, accept what's happening, and add to it. Coaching encourages and is a foundation of heart culture.

You have to listen and observe first to understand where people are coming from. Only then can you meet people where they are. You wouldn't say to an infant, "Stop crawling on the floor, get up and walk." The infant hasn't developed the right skills yet. Coaching is care. It asks the question "How can we go forward from here?" Heart doesn't rush to judgment.

Calm conveys confidence. Personal development starts with simple tools like MBTI. We use many other tools to develop self-awareness. Being centered is to be "in yourself," not distracted by a thousand competing thoughts that knock you off balance. Being centered is an awareness of what is happening right now: being present. Meditation for me is just peace and quiet. I'm in a place to accept what thoughts and feelings are present.

TANYA: Meditation for me is a reminder to stay in the heart, to observe what's going on and not to let negative thoughts get the better of me. It helps me maintain calm. Occasional stress isn't a bad thing. It's a necessary part of life. The body mobilizes to meet an unusual challenge. And this is the important part: then you need rest in order to recover. But it's long-term stress that becomes toxic. When you have no calm and nurturing place to retreat to, no place to recharge your batteries, stress becomes corrosive. Chronic stress causes all sorts of personal, medical, psychological, and organizational problems.

BUTCH: CEOs struggle every day with the results of chronic stress in the organization. Drama is the norm. They run after this, and do that, and this unconscious behavior only adds to the problem. Our focus is to make everything calmer than it was. Most things aren't that critical and can be taken care of. This attitude changes the whole organization and it changes you. When you, as leader, maintain genuine calm and you don't have daily panics, you feel better. People notice. It's completely different.

TANYA: Many styles of meditative exercises are now available. That's another example of remarkable change! Whether yoga, or mindfulness, it's the quiet time alone with yourself that matters.

Even if the concept of sitting with yourself looking inward is foreign to you, it doesn't matter. Quiet time as simple as observing your breath going in and out is enough.

Jon Kabat-Zinn pioneered Mindfulness Based Stress Reduction in 1979. Using techniques from various meditative disciplines, he designed ways of working with medical patients to cope with their pain, anxiety, and physical illnesses. He describes a state called "moment-to-moment awareness" that can arise.

When we worked with Susanne Cook-Greuter, she began meetings of associates with "120 seconds of mindfulness." At first, I was concerned about how people would respond. I think most of the other leaders were, too. Thankfully, we had Butch. His tranquil attitude calmed us all.

People were instructed to sit quietly, notice their breathing, and let their thoughts come into the present moment. This was quite a departure for some folks. We saw how this simple practice changed the atmosphere.

Some people consider meditation as a particular religious practice. It is not. Herbert Benson, MD, is the Mind Body Medicine Professor of Medicine, Harvard Medical School. His ground-breaking book, *The Relaxation Response*, shows how to calm yourself. It has no religious connection, and he calls meditation by another name. It's hard in the business environment to talk even about spirituality. It's easier to talk about character development.

BUTCH: I view character as external and spiritual as internal. Character is what others see. Spiritual is what you experience. Spiritual is what you are. One is an external face and one is an internal face.

More people are realizing that meditation, or mindfulness, isn't religiously threatening. More businesses and CEOs are using it. There are all kinds of projects and companies out there who are doing this. The president of Aetna Insurance—amazing—he's fully out with it. "I'm meditating and you're going to do it too if you want to be a leader here."

We use it. It changes everything.

The easiest way to start is to simply watch your breath for two minutes. Watching your breath takes you in whether you want to go in or not. If you're watching your breath, you get there.

Your mind is active. Thoughts are going to come. Don't be judgmental of your mind. Whatever comes up, just say, "That's nice. I appreciate the thought." Just accept what's there and move back to watching your breath.

TANYA: You have to start with yourself, which we did when we began working with CCL. That's actually what opened all this up.

Meditation is working on yourself by looking at what's going on internally. You start by recognizing your own in-the-moment experience. As you gain greater knowledge of your self-observations, you come to learn to understand other people, too. It's a method of becoming fully adult—of becoming mature. We moved this forward with the idea of know yourself first.

Cindy Wigglesworth is writing on spiritual quotient and has gone a long way toward removing religion from mindfulness. You can talk about involvement. You can talk about leadership levels. These help people to become more aware of how they're perceived in the world and how they see themselves. Everyone can understand the value of unruffled personal calm, especially under difficult conditions.

BUTCH: We were evolving along with the company. We often just followed our curiosity about higher levels of development. We said to ourselves, "I'm going to get better and change and learn. Let's find out what this is all about. Let's just try it and see if it works." Tanya and I tried meditation, and it continues to work for us. It helps us be more understanding, patient, and calmer than we've ever been. And that's a good place to operate from.

Heart Is Open

Everything in life is an experiment. There are no guarantees. Organic transformation requires breaking apart what exists. The chrysalis drops away and a butterfly appears. An egg cracks and life emerges. The snake sheds its skin as it grows larger. While shedding, the snake is vulnerable to predators. This risk is natural and must be faced in order to evolve. Fear of the unknown is normal. But do you want that to hold you back?

BUTCH: Manufacturing clients usually turn to a coach or a consultant when there's something going wrong, or they can't clearly see the way forward. Engagements are expected to be transactional, like here's a problem; find out how to fix it. This might also be a starting point of transformation. Small changes can have a big effect.

TANYA: We've used some visualization techniques for deepening awareness of how thoughts impact feeling and behavior. But we've never used the words spiritual or meditation. We took baby steps with introducing a 120-second mindfulness exercise. We often restart meetings from break time and lunches using the singing bowl. It's a very healing vibrational tone. It has a really nice effect on bringing people back together.

Two minutes is all AT was ready for at the time, and that's okay. Too much too soon causes resistance. Often new behaviors need time to become habits, and then you can move on to something deeper. You need time for fresh behavior to emerge from each developmental insight.

BUTCH: It's a matter of readiness. You have to build the trust first.

Goodbye, We Love You

In August 2007, AT Carbide de México became a subsidiary of AT. By 2010, the plant was continually improving processes and cycle times. Production increased. Delivery times were shorter. Associates were continually improving communication skills, expanding their range of capabilities, developing new procedures and new products. By 2011, operating margin improved over the previous year. But by late 2012, due to low Chinese prices, cancelled orders and high fixed expenses for the level of production, the plant was forced to shut down. C.B., the AT Carbide de México associate, tells her story:

The future for AT Carbide de México was not encouraging. It [the closing] was without doubt a shock, but perfectly understandable. We couldn't hold back our tears, losing this place where we laughed, cried, shared, and enjoyed. It had become our second home and our second family.

Before belonging to AT, the plant was dark and somewhat rundown. Employees were just surviving, staying in their comfort zone. It became a brightly illuminated plant, with life and movement, remodeled from the entrance to the bathrooms; and most importantly with transformed associates inside willing to shape the world to make it better.

Today, we are not the same. We have evolved thanks to your (Butch's) influence. We truly appreciate your guidance and support. You leave Mexico a great legacy and you will always be in our hearts.

Heart Is Appreciative

BUTCH: I get great satisfaction in seeing how far people have come, how much they have embraced heart culture, and how much they have developed in response to their environment. And they continue to grow.

I heard from the people in Mexico: "You taught me to have a better job. I thank you. Your three years here was worth it. I learned so much about myself and about business. I was now capable of getting a job and a having a better family life."

It's significant to me every time I hear somebody say "It was really cool what we did. It meant something to me. It changed me. It helped me. You didn't force it. You offered it to me. It was my choice and I took it."

These are the things that stay with me and push me forward.

TANYA: About an hour after one of our annual kick-off meetings, a guy from our engineering process ran up and said, "I just want you to know that was an awesome meeting. I've been here over 10 years and I love hearing about and knowing that we continue to evolve. It's so exciting."

I often remember that moment in the cafeteria. It reminds me of how thrilling it is to be a part of such an evolutionary organization. I've received many individual thank-you's over the years; personal gratitude for providing an environment for growth or an emotionally safe place. It feels good when you've made a positive difference in another person's well-being. People have told me, "You saved my marriage."

This comes from work! It makes me want to keep doing it.

BUTCH: When someone tells another person that you did something they thought was really cool, and it comes to you third-hand, it's even more powerful. Then you know what you're doing is taking on a life of its own. It's *sticky*. It's talked about. It's part of the culture. People are spreading the word and building the community wider, broader, and deeper.

We talked earlier about the community coming together spontaneously when someone is sick. That's a big high because it didn't come from me. It's a reflection of a self-organizing system. It's an environment where people connect with each other. This generates caring. So these free acts are more encouraging and admirable than if I had said, "You should go and help that person." Associates didn't have to help each other. It came from their hearts, from a feeling of connection and empathy.

Our Manufacturing with Heart experiment came from just doing. It wasn't a programmed event. We didn't measure it. We just observed what was unfolding (being) and moved from there.

It was feeling and direction. As we said earlier, leadership is a never-ending practice. It is without beginning, middle or end. It is being and doing, doing and being.

TANYA: We continually work to develop ourselves as individuals, as associates, and with our teams, our company, our industry, and the world. Here we are, just a small company making a positive difference.

Big Heart

Old restrictions drop away as associates assimilate heart culture. More functional behavior appears. Susanne Cook-Greuter teaches about stages of adult development. Her model aligns capacity for love with three stages of awareness.

Her stages are pre-conventional, conventional, and post-conventional. There is not enough space to go into the model in detail here, but it works like this: As a person transcends and includes each stage, their capacity for love increases along with their awareness of themselves and others. Awareness and heart are intertwined.

Evolution of heart is more uncovering than creating. Natural growth moves in all directions, both vertically and horizontally. In the same way, capacity for love increases with awareness, so self-development positively impacts group behavior.

Vertical development progresses as each person knows themselves better. They gain wider perspective as their self-sense deepens. They come to trust and believe in the heart model, and grow into greater self-confidence. Heart deepens experience.

Horizontal development is a result of vertical development. It's inter-personal and shows up as care and teaching from associate to associate. A culture of respect and the freedom to experiment make development possible. The big payoff is how every associate matures in their ability to communicate, and give to one another. Heart is connection.

Heart culture merges left brain and right brain functions, masculine and feminine creative energies, intelligence quotient and emotional quotient, and head and heart. This meeting is the living reality of *yin* and *yang*, opposites folded together into a holistic unity.

A manufacturing company with heart is a natural expression of health and growth. We've come a long way from the dark and squalid factories of the 19th century. Machine mind is still common today, but is giving way to new habits of being as leaders understand more of themselves and what's possible. Sustainable leadership in the 21st century has to embrace deep human understanding. As barriers are breaking down between *us* and *them*, leadership needs greater awareness of developmental cycles of doing and being, insights and gestation leading to new levels of functionality.

Your workplace can transcend into an exciting laboratory of care, productivity, and collective satisfaction. Working people become whole. Day-to-day routine takes on a higher purpose.

At last, heart and human feeling are finding their rightful place in collective human activity.

Heartbeat
- Heart dares
- Heart is open to new experience
- Heart unifies opposites
- Heart doesn't rush to judgment
- Heart deepens experience
- Heart is connection
- Heart is calm
- Heart is open
- Heart appreciates
- Heart expands and includes

Part Two

Transformation

13 Steps Toward Transformation

1. Get Flatter, Go Further

Change from traditional to process-centered organization

What

Traditional manufacturing companies are organized around product lines. Each product line has its own customer service, sales, management, etc., with a clear chain of command, many time-consuming rules, and managers who administer them. As long as conditions remain the same (which they never seem to do) traditional organizations can be efficient.

Process-centered organizations (PCOs) are aligned around processes, i.e., a collection of sequential tasks, such as finance, machining, or assembly. Teams are organized by process for all products. For example, finance teams work within the finance process. Leading each process is a process engineer and coach.

PCOs flatten the traditional hierarchy, discarding layers of management and titles in favor of process engineers, coaches, and associates (*See Chapter 5*).

Why

Traditional structures are vulnerable to rapid change and increasingly become unattractive to a 21st century workforce. In its extreme form, the traditional hierarchy is authoritarian. When that happens people are afraid to offer suggestions for improvement. Innovation suffers when a company fails to engage the collective wisdom of its people. In the traditional structure each product line can be unaware of others, causing redundancies and inefficiencies.

By contrast, PCO functions at a higher developmental level. Individuals learn more about and understand themselves and other people better, resulting in effective communication. PCO fosters collective creativity because it encourages teams to make their own decisions. Process engineers and coaches are responsible for removing barriers preventing associates from doing their jobs well. Environments of care and autonomy foster long-term loyalty, pride, and gratitude. Customers, the company, and associates win.

2. Jump around

Stop focusing just on fixed tasks and move to the work

What

Fixed tasks are mechanical operations. Traditionally, people were only trained for one job. They were required to complete simple and repetitive tasks with little understanding of the bigger process in which they worked.

Move to the work is where cross-trained individuals understand the whole process and their place in it. People have read the Goal and understand how bottlenecks occur and how to address them.

Why

Today repetitive, task-based skills are the domain of robots. Any failure in a task-based line will create bottlenecks resulting in breakdown, decreased productivity, and delays. Traditional hierarchies tend toward cultures of secrecy and fear so people are stressed, disengaged, or alienated.

Move to the work increases productivity. Move to the work expands associates' capabilities and awareness of the whole process-centered organization. They can look in front of them and behind and move to where they're needed. Associates have more autonomy. By learning more and better skills, they increase value to themselves and the company. Move to the work demonstrates a company's agility. It is less vulnerable to weak links and therefore more resilient and robust (*See Chapter 5*).

3. Stop approving

Abandon manager approvals in favor of employee accountability

What

Manager approvals are procedures for documenting requests, making judgments to approve or deny allocation of funds.

Employee accountability doesn't need manager approvals. Budgets are allocated to teams so they can make their own decisions.

Why

Manager approvals have many layers. They're cumbersome and subject to communication errors. Filling out paperwork, even if it's online, can be an unnecessary habit. Managers are forced to make judgments. Almost always people's requests for manager approvals are approved.

A weakness with manager-approved purchases is that they remove responsibility for associates to think about the cost of what they're requesting.

Employee accountability works on the basis of trust and competency. In our experience people buy only what's needed. Abandoning the approval process frees time and speeds production. When people are treated as adults they usually respond that way. This has a positive impact on the whole organization. Having autonomy with accountability in one area is more likely to help people act responsibly in other areas.

"Just go get what you need when you need it" is an expression of trust and effectiveness.

4. Say goodbye to employee reviews

Replace employee reviews with individual development plans.

What

Employee reviews look backward. They are judgments; assessments of past performance.

Individual associate development plans (IADPs) look forward. Their purpose is to help associates realize their future potential in both hard and soft skills.

Why

Only looking backward does little to prepare for an ever-changing environment. There is value to looking at past performance, but it shouldn't stop there. What's missing with performance reviews is preparation and support for learning what hasn't yet been mastered.

IADPs are designed for individuals and aligned with process goals. Along with coaches and process engineers, IADPs offer continual support to help associates learn rather than only judge past performance.

5. Be here now

Let go of attendance policies. Create attendance guidelines

What

Attendance policies specify mandatory rules for being at work, and under what conditions employees can work overtime, take sick time, personal days, and vacation.

Attendance guidelines communicate the needs of the company, what's expected from associates, and how to talk about their individual needs with their teams, process engineers, and coaches.

Why

Over the last 100 years, manufacturing companies have progressively added more restrictions. Policing attendance takes time and leads to an absurdity: tracking the time it takes to track time.

Attendance policy manuals can run to 50 pages or more of things employees can't do. Replace time tracking with clear communication of expectations.

Simplify: Replace a long list of restrictions with a short list of expectations. Associates are expected to be on time for shifts. If they can't make it, they should let people know.

In a culture of trust you can get rid of attendance policy, free up administrative time, and make people feel more responsible and respected. Trust generates loyalty and dedication.

6. Stop playing the budget game

Retire top-down budgeting. Teach collaborative budgeting

What

There are two players in the top-down budgeting game: executive and middle managers. Executives demand unrealistic budget tightening. Middle managers pad their needs to compensate.

Collaborative budgeting seeks input from everyone. Each process team submits their priorities. Budgets are project driven and outcome driven.

Why

Each party in the top-down budgeting game knows the other is lying. Now time-wasting negotiations commence. Leadership makes across-the-board percentage cuts reducing everyone's ability to function at an optimal level.

Collaborative budgeting is a result of input from everyone. All people on the shop floor have practical assessments of what they need to do their jobs for the coming year. Process groups decide on their priorities among themselves. Instead of across-the-board cuts, some projects are abandoned, leaving those which are selected to be fully funded (*See Chapter 5*).

7. Put your oxygen mask on first

The customer is number one; but you must balance the needs of the customer with the welfare of the company, associates and other stakeholders.

What

The customer is number one: Business is there to serve customer needs, but not when those needs damage the health of the company.

Customer needs should be integrated among customer, company, associates, and other stakeholders.

Why

"The customer is always right" is a slogan from London's Selfridges Department Store in an early 20th-century publicity campaign. The idea stuck. But in its extreme form it hurts everyone, and ultimately the customer when unprofitable negotiations lead to bankruptcy. If customers are always right, they can buy at whatever price they choose and behave badly.

Every company is focused on helping customers. Decision making, such as whether to take on new projects, should be made with respect to capabilities, all work in progress, and the needs of other stakeholders. Suppliers must beware of customers demanding pricing, delivery, and terms that are unprofitable, cause delays, or interfere with current projects. Associates are trained to negotiate with buyers based on their holistic understanding of operations and productions limits (*See Chapter 5*).

8. Throw away what you don't need

Employee policies to employee guidebook

What

An employee policy handbook contains legal requirements, rules, and alienating restrictions.

An employee guidebook communicates goals and expectations of the company. While retaining legal requirements, its purpose is to make people feel part of the company and advise them on what they can do, rather than what they can't do.

Why

Policies are necessary, but they limit action. Employee policy handbooks are cumbersome, take time to maintain, and waste administrative effort. Except for those legally required, many policies are without value. Moreover, language in employee policy handbooks is harsh, demanding, and alienating. Without trust there can only be rules and surveillance.

An employee guidebook gives associates an understanding of the background of the company, and their place in it. By use of friendly, functional, and inclusive language, a guidebook communicates how the company is structured, what the company is doing for the associate, and what the company expects in return. Legal requirements are inserted at the end of the book. Trust frees resources (*See Chapter 6*).

9. Trust in transparency

Arbitrary pay to compensation plans

What

Pay is arbitrary and secret. Compensation plans match pay within nationally published pay ranges.

Why

Rumors grow in the dark. When pay is secret, employees imagine other people and departments are being better compensated than they are. Secrecy breeds dissent and dissatisfaction.

People are more concerned about fairness than absolute numbers. However, when people want more money it's an opportunity to coach. Discuss what would be necessary for an employee to increase their value to the company through education, skill acquisition, training, and individual associate development plans (IADP).

Transparency fosters trust. Conduct surveys to ensure associates are being properly paid. Communicate nationally published pay ranges to everyone.

10. Not just for those at the top

Leadership development to employee development plans

What

Leadership development is the norm for management.

Employee development plans expand leadership development to everyone in the company.

Why

Your company benefits when all the people within it function at higher levels. When people have more awareness of themselves, initially through MBTI®, they become better listeners and so communicate more skillfully with their peers.

Associates can take on more responsibility and learn a wider range of tasks through development plans. As people learn greater respect for others and recognize their own dignity, teams function more effectively. Development plans lead to greater awareness of the needs of individuals and common corporate goals.

11. It's the way you say it

Culture damaging language to culture building language

What

Word choice is a function of culture. Culture damaging language describes what happens when the words we use are unwittingly toxic.

Awareness of how words impact people is the foundation of culture building language.

Why

Language conveys emotional meaning. The words you use can build or destroy culture. For example, "you people" disconnects the "superior" speaker from listeners. This phrase creates divisions. The word "mandatory" carries with it the possibility of punishment for non-compliance. There is no negotiating with mandatory.

Collaborative language allows people to communicate in positive ways compatible with the direction of company goals (*See Chapters 4 and Appendix 1*).

12. Stop hiring for skills only

Focus on skills to focus on culture

What

Traditional companies have limited themselves by hiring and promoting people based solely on skill sets.

By focusing on culture, the whole company benefits.

Why

Exceptional performance in a position was rewarded by promotions to higher-level jobs individuals may have been poorly suited to, often without necessary cultural support for learning. The Peter Principle: Why things always go wrong, by Laurence J. Peter, is a witty book that's main message is that people are promoted beyond the level of their competence.

Every company has a culture, whether it's been designed and developed, or it just happened. Problems occur when cultural support is missing. When management is only interested in hard metrics, it can easily turn a blind eye to workplace bullying. In such a culture people try to protect themselves, their jobs, and bargain for salary and benefits by hoarding knowledge. This sort of organization has a learning disability.

Culture matters. Task skills are easier to teach than people development. Culture is the collective attitudes and behaviors of people within a company. By developing an atmosphere of trust with shared learning, cross-training, and support as norms, companies respond to rapid change, lower workforce stress, and create a more congenial workplace.

13. Abandon recognition programs

Recognition programs to celebrations

What

Recognitions programs are bureaucratic and formal. They publically recognize individual achievement.

Celebrations are collective events recognizing inclusive group effort.

Why

Most people want to be sincerely appreciated for what they do. Public recognition of individuals can cause jealousies. Recognition programs lack sincerity. They are an obligation and one more administrative task to be completed. Genuine feeling is usually missing.

Often recognition programs are put in place in response to poor showings in employee surveys. They motivate people only for what's on the reward list. Rewards are transactional. Genuine private and spontaneous appreciation can have a transformational effect (*See Chapter 6*).

Celebrations can be informal birthday parties, collective dinners, or annual events where everyone learns about what and how the company is doing.

Part Three
Heartbeats

Heartbeats: A Quick Guide

We know you're busy. That's why you're reading this section first. This is a quick reminder-guide as food for thought based on the main ideas in this book. This is a big conceptual meal and we don't want you to get indigestion. You may not want to rush through all of these items in one sitting. We've structured this section on the "Heartbeat" lists at the end of each chapter.

We hope this guide will stimulate your thinking. We're advocating for transformational change, not quick fixes. Every company is different. We find that our clients' exact needs and direction emerge through analysis and discussion.

Chapter 1: Our World

Our manufacturing world is changing fast

1. Resilience and agility are crucial to survival.

2. You'd better have some money to so you can do what you need to do when you need to do it.

3. Don't overextend your company. Avoid deep leveraging. Where possible, join sustained internal growth to growth

through acquisitions, diversification of markets, distribution channels, customers, and product lines to ensure long-term financial stability.

4. Be prepared. Regularly assess and adjust internal structures to maximize your company's flexibility.

5. Don't waste your time getting lean; just be agile. Too many people stop at lean. Lean is doing what you have to do today. Agile is doing what you have to do for tomorrow.

6. Resilience = taking care of yourself in body, mind, and spirit. Be ready to step back and say, "Whoa."

7. For more on heart, see www.mindful.org.

Think holistically

1. First understand yourself, and how you fit into the picture. Then take your place as a person in the picture helping to make the picture.

2. Beliefs, organization, technology, and culture together support employee development.

3. Align CEO, leaders, and employees through daily communication, accessible information.

4. Learning is the work.

5. People want to contribute. Support them, coach them, teach them, encourage them, and reward them.

Trust culture + PCO leads to Manufacturing with Heart

1. Everything starts with you.

2. Give trust 10:1 odds.

3. Radiate trust in all directions.

4. A trusting atmosphere creates wonders.

5. PCO opens up the arena for individual creativity to play.

6. Develop unwavering trust in a better world.

Small manufacturing organizations have the advantage

1. You're lucky to be a cheetah, not an elephant.

2. Your company size lets you touch everyone. Make sure all communications drive direction, alignment, and commitment.

3. Get to know everyone. Let them know you.

4. Know that every employee has a good idea. Ask and listen.

5. Small size = fewer constraints = easier change.

Policy needs to match intentions

1. Simplify and support.

2. Get rid of titles to reduce tension and competition.

3. Match attendance policies to the real world of employee's lives.

4. Trustworthy employees don't need surveillance.

Positive culture change is possible: expect resistance

1. Listen with empathy to employee fears, and keep moving forward.

2. Communicate the "why."

3. Identify and coach passive resistance. Recognize that some employees may need to leave.

4. Nobody says change is easy.

5. Believe in your vision and carry on.

Millennials need a different kind of workplace

1. Find out what your employees want. You might be surprised.

2. Build around purpose. Tell everyone what it is.

3. Tyranny is out.

4. Attract, train, and retain with work/life balance, autonomy, career development, and meaningful work.

New possibilities start with you

1. For new possibilities you have to overcome the inertia of what is now. To do this you need to change something.

2. Begin by looking at where you are.

3. Which unrealized possibilities do you want for your company?

4. What problems need fixing?

5. Are you ready for change?

6. Are you ready to work with the challenges of change?

7. How can you be a better leader?

8. Would you like to influence your world for good?

9. Can you ask for help to support your transition?

10. How open is your company to new thinking?

11. Do you trust your employees?

12. Do you believe in happiness at work?

13. Self-development takes courage and perseverance. The payoff is huge.

14. You've already started. What's next?

Chapter 2: Beliefs

Make sure your beliefs are in sync with heart-centered goals

1. Beliefs drive thought, feeling, and action.
2. See if your beliefs are in sync with where you want to go. If they're not, you'll confuse yourself and everybody else.
3. Do a gut check. Do your beliefs feel right? Do they all point to heart, or do you see conflicts?
4. Are your beliefs big enough to hold the world you imagine?

Your beliefs set the tone of your company

1. Be transparent. Tell people how you feel and what you're doing. Make your beliefs public.
2. Show how your beliefs play out through your actions.
3. Caring comes from inside. People know when you're faking it.

Believe in your employees' creativity

1. You're smart, with good ideas. Imagine what 500 focused, energized people like you could accomplish together.
2. Implement your employees' suggestions – even when you might see a better way. This creates trust, which leads to more ideas. (See all hands on deck story in Chapter 7.)
3. Provide an enriched environment full of personal and process learning options. Then stand back and see what happens.

Make sure everyone understands your positive beliefs

1. Keep listening and talking.
2. Keep your leadership team listening and talking.

3. Ask employees where they feel unheard. (See story about collecting ideas in Chapter 6.)

Believe in constant communication

1. Answer all questions. Sometimes the answer is "No."

2. Heart language generates heart culture.

3. Talking together is where minds and hearts touch. Always be mindful of the power of your opportunity for caring, listening, and showing.

4. Why do we need to share information?

5. Am I giving information freely to others?

6. Do I receive information with an open mind?

7. Do I ask questions when I don't understand?

8. Do I have the right information to get the job done?

Share holistic beliefs with all stakeholders

1. Expand the effects of heart-centered by living it with vendors, customers, and community.

2. Holding tight to respectful action with all employees shows stakeholders you mean what you say.

3. Your company becomes a transmitter of caring; everyone feels it. (*See Chapter 7*)

Chapter 3: Leading from the Heart

Know yourself

1. Leadership is based on values; be clear about what they are.
2. When you know yourself fully, the force of your being communicates what you want to say.
3. Wonderful tools are available to help you and your leaders understand self and others.
4. Transparency generates heart.

Be patient with everyone, especially yourself

1. Wherever you are is the perfect place to start.
2. Head learning is fast. "Being" learning takes time. Think of yourself as a tree moving upward and outward. The bigger you are, the more shade you provide.
3. Practice on yourself the qualities you're developing with others.

Invest in your self-development first

You'll feel much better as you let go of ways that don't serve the heart vision. This turns out to be fun.

1. You're the warrior. People look to you for strength, courage, and generosity.
2. It's hard at first, but the payoffs from self-knowledge are irreplaceable.

Everyone can practice the art of leadership

1. It happens. Believe it. 500 leaders.

2. When money's off the table, people seek autonomy, challenge, and creativity. This works to your company's advantage.

3. Your employees will love you for nurturing their own leadership.

Leadership is an ongoing way of being, not a means to an end

1. "Being" influences more than talking because "presence" is clearly visible.

2. Predicting the future is impossible. There's only now to work your magic.

3. Become all you want to be, then provide the same opportunities for your employees.

Observe what's happening right now

1. Stop, look, and listen.

2. See from multiple perspectives: AQAL

3. Your task is to hold the big external vision for your company. Can you add personal internal vision? (*See Chapter 7*)

4. Learn a whole new world of information to work with. What does it feel like to be in finance? Production? Leadership?

5. What's the emotional tone of your company? Are people happy?

6. Do you promote work-life balance for everyone by demonstrating it yourself?

Cultivate harmony

1. Check for alignment of values, principles and habits.

2. Align means fit together smoothly. When positive energy runs from beliefs through habits, obstacles disappear.

3. You can see, hear, and feel disharmony. You have the power to change it.

4. Start by telling people what you see. Offer options.

Simplify as much as you can, but not too much

1. Hold every rule to a high standard of utility. Keep the ones that make sense for the 80 percent of your employees who are trustworthy.

2. It feels great to de-clutter.

3. Create space and see what emerges.

4. Don't put things in that you have to take out. Think through a whole process so you don't build in conflicts.

Demonstrate care

1. Smooth the path, remove obstacles.

2. The heart atmosphere you create improves employees' lives, both at work and at home.

3. As an ad for teachers says, "You don't need to be famous to be remembered." Employees never forget a boss who generates well-being.

4. Creativity longs to emerge. You build a stimulating workplace, then step back.

Chapter 4: Shift Happens

Experiment and see what happens

1. Incremental is a beautiful word. Take small steps.

2. Try stuff. Then watch, listen, feel into it.

3. Talk about the excitement and benefits that emerge.

4. A secure, safe environment reduces natural anxiety generated by change.

Tolerate not knowing

1. Risk means without a guarantee. You take a chance. Just don't wager the whole farm.

2. Just being alive is risky. We pretend it isn't. Look for the exhilaration in chaos.

3. Center yourself in whatever works for you. You're the steady rock in a sea of change (*See Chapter 7*)

Know the why

1. When employees understand what you're trying to achieve; they want to help you. Many ideas will emerge.

2. Sharing the "why" creates a blueprint for action.

3. People feel trusted when you involve them in big picture decisions.

Communicate, communicate, communicate

1. Talk continually about what you're trying to achieve.

2. Talk to everyone gently and persuasively about heart culture. Listen to their concerns. Address these specifically.

3. Show people examples of what's possible. There's plenty to point to now.

4. People talk. Get the grapevine on board with your messages.

5. Ask questions.

6. Why do we need to share information?

7. Am I giving the right information freely to others?

8. Do I receive information with an open mind?

9. Do I ask questions when I don't understand?

10. Do I have the right information to get the job done?

Language matters

1. Align the power of words with the power of your vision.

2. Teach everyone how to communicate respectfully.

3. Use words like appreciate, thank you, how's your work going?

4. Taking away the hierarchy of titles creates a whole new playing field.

5. When everyone is an associate, cooperation can replace competition.

Lower stress, boost productivity

1. Long-term stress kills brain cells.

2. Manageable stress is fun. We call it a "challenge." It grows new brain connections. Think of golf.

3. Challenge generates energy by releasing norepinephrine in the brain. This improves mood and creativity.

4. Your health insurance costs go down when people feel better and take care of themselves.

Care

1. Genuine caring is the best tool you've got. It's also the right way to be.

2. You're in a unique position to generate an oasis of care. How far can you take it?

3. Care leads your business to conscious capitalism. This is how we change the world: One company at a time.

Chapter 5: Collective Creativity

Creative minds are curious

1. Encourage questions. Questions are the currency of thinking. Thought produces solutions. You never know who's going to come up with a great idea.

2. You can stimulate originality by building an enjoyable, inspiring workplace.

3. Support "Learning is the work."

Corporate structures either prevent or encourage collective creativity

1. A process-centered workplace replaces mind-numbing routine with learning and flexibility.

2. Providing employees with easy access to information speeds up decisions and actions.

3. Go for the gold. Build in the best structures known to arouse productivity. You win, everyone wins.

Higher individual levels of development make for better group interactions

1. Employees developed in self-understanding, good communication, and capable of multiple tasks boost productivity.

2. Product, ideas, self-correcting discipline, self-direction, and confidence are traits of effective autonomous groups.

3. People want to belong. Create the right environment.

How decisions are made is more important than outcomes

1. Use your 500 leaders. Share all pertinent information. Give a nod to known unknowns, and unknown unknowns. Relax.

2. PCO and a learning culture increase productivity. Trust in this.

3. When things get crazy, stay calm. Keep moving. Use your 500 leaders.

4. Rely on your informed, alert systems to catch problems. 500 leaders have 1,000 eyes.

Groups are more likely to make accurate predictions than individuals

1. Listen to the wisdom of the crowd.

2. What emerges from the minds of your informed people is as close as you can get to reality.

3. You can create your own cutting-edge manufacturing university.

4. Active group participation makes people feel included.

5. Encourage everyone to contribute toward high-level planning.

A working laboratory is a place to try something different

1. In a learning culture your whole company becomes R&D.

2. Human creativity is a spontaneous gift to be cultivated with freedom.

3. Employees appreciate being able to use their skills to contribute to their organization.

Genuine recognition makes a positive difference

1. As a small to mid-sized manufacturer, you have the advantage of knowing everyone's name. Say "Bob, great job with that product. Thank you." Catch people doing things well, and commend them.

2. One-on-one, unscripted personal recognition for a job well done is better than a public ceremony.

3. Consistency and sincerity are the pillars of recognition.

Spontaneous groups get things done

1. Communities of Practice are short-term groups bringing together people from different processes for a specific purpose.

2. Dedicated employees choosing to focus together on a unique project is at the top of what can be achieved in the learning culture.

3. Motivated groups are incubators to solve problems or develop a new product.

4. Communities of practice are a great way for employees to try out new tasks.

5. They bring together people from all parts of the company, reducing "us and them" barriers.

Sincere appreciation creates a sense of belonging

1. Don't be reluctant to show and tell your employees how grateful you are for their good work. This creates real loyalty.

2. A leader who cares about employees can do great good in the workplace.

3. Who doesn't crave appreciation? Generate a positive feedback loop with your words and actions.

Apprentice try-out programs

1. Apprentice programs give people a chance to try new jobs.

2. People gain a realistic appreciation of their current roles, other roles, people and groups.

3. Some of our apprentices loved taking on a new role in the company and making a permanent change.

4. Others had a valuable experience in another department that sent them happily back to their old jobs.

5. Everyone's knowledge expanded and we all won.

Communities of care

1. As people learn and grow together, genuine care for each other develops.

2. Employees spontaneously help each other through personal crises.

3. A positive and productive workplace reaches deep levels of heart connection.

Creativity is in all of us

1. Your commitment to supporting your employees' freedom to learn, evolve, and make decisions is the greatest gift you can offer them.

2. An office worker comes up with a unique product design. A line technician becomes a gifted teacher. Working together, people from different departments find ways to significantly reduce costs.

3. Employee polls show that meaningful work is a primary need and motivator.

Chapter 6: Trust

A culture of trust doesn't waste resources on unnecessary surveillance and metrics

1. Trusted employees don't have to be watched. The time saved is a huge resource.

2. Most employees are reliable. Unnecessary rules are for the few who aren't.

3. "How many can you make?" This works better than "Make 14."

Actions speak louder than words

1. DWYSYWD is the fastest way to gain trust.

2. Doing what you said you would do demonstrates reliability.

3. People judge lack of follow-through as insincerity. They're right.

4. Anyone can be a saint alone in their room. It's what you DO when you come out and face real people and real challenges that's your measure.

Be consistent. Show you're sincere

1. Reliable, steady, dependable, constant, unswerving—all of these mean "sincere".

2. Consistency means coming through time after time. The time element is what you build with.

3. Having a solid track record speaks for itself.

Mistakes are inevitable

1. Accept consequences of all of your actions. Apologize and make amends when necessary.

2. Demonstrate how you want everyone else to act.

3. It's hard to be vulnerable, but brilliantly human.

4. A mistake is usually just trying something new.

5. Stop judging yourself. Only then does not judging others become easier.

Care is taking into account everyone's interests

1. Furthering your employees' and stakeholders' welfare is an honor unique to a servant leader.

2. Think of a holon. (*See Chapter 1*) Your company is big holon. Every employee is small holon.

3. Every small, healthy holon contributes to greater complexity of function of the larger holon.

Trust is demonstrated through openness

1. When you have nothing to hide, it's easy to be open.

2. Openness demonstrates confidence in yourself, others, and the world. It's a good way to live. It's relaxing.

3. Sharing your thoughts and building collective understanding relaxes other people.

Transparency is the antidote to the rumor mill

1. Answer all questions clearly and honestly.

2. Tell people how you need them to ask to be sure you hear everything.

3. Who's generating rumors? Talk to them especially. Bring them over to your way of thinking. Make the rumor mill your friend.

Competence isn't just skill and knowledge

1. Competence includes the willingness and ability to learn.

2. Learning moves people and organizations forward. Love of learning shows enthusiasm, agility, and enjoyment.

3. Hire for excitement about learning. These are the people who will keep your business alive.

4. Manufacturing universities are the cutting edge of commerce.

Trust has boundaries

1. Examine trust violations from all five trust perspectives before taking action.

2. Ask: Have you pushed risk-taking too far?

3. Ask: Were you frightened your needs would not be met?

4. Ask: Do you need more training?

5. Ask: Do you understand the importance of doing what you said you would do?

6. Ask: What was the intention behind your action?

First, give people the benefit of the doubt

1. Your natural state is belief in the integrity of others.

2. Your company structure and culture embodies your current level of trust.

3. Being slow to judge allows misunderstanding to come to light.

4. Most people have integrity.

Communicate trust through word choice

1. Speaking respectfully communicates humility, a mark of the servant leader.

2. Clear messages to employees about your expectations show you trust that they're capable.

3. If you doubt your communication skills, get some training. Solicit feedback. Intention is what matters.

Be realistic

1. Building trust takes time and stamina.

2. There's no instant "trust" switch.

3. Stamina keeps you in for the long haul. "Never give in," as Churchill said. He was frighteningly energetic.

4. Take care of yourself. Find time for enjoyment, exercise, meditation. This puts you in the positive zone.

5. Know today is the day everything comes together. This may take many days.

Pay attention to your intentions, and those of others

1. Find time for daily reflection. Check in to be sure you're on track.

2. Can you risk trusting other people?

3. Intention is the indicator of an employee's good fit with heart culture.

Create an environment where people feel safe

1. Safe = Growth. Fear shuts down trust, creativity, and enjoyment.

2. Safe = Less control. Freedom means you stand back a little. Things are not always done the way you would do them. This is good.

3. Safe = Nontoxic. You're creating a work environment free from the toxins of greed, tyranny, disrespect, and lethargy. Lucky you. Lucky staff. Lucky world.

Chapter 7: Heart Culture

Heart dares

1. It's a true friendship: the positive, learning organization and employees on fire to grow.

2. When inspired employees discover what's being offered, they feel they've come home.

3. Building heart culture is a unique undertaking.

4. Daring to believe in what's possible is your engine of growth.

Heart unifies opposites

1. "Us and them" melts as people find commonality in creating together.

2. Hard manufacturing and soft people skills go really well together.

Heart deepens experience

1. Taking down hierarchies, providing learning opportunities, paying good wages, supporting self-care all transform people's lives.

2. When boundaries are removed, the human spirit can soar. Happiness and productivity are a natural result.

3. Here people look after each other, enjoy their work, and spontaneously express gratitude.

Heart is connection

1. Coaches and process engineers connect with employees' desire to improve. Patiently helping to remove obstacles to better functioning connects coach to employee, employee to task and company. A positive web of engagement emerges.

2. When it's crunch time, you get to see the agility of heart in action.

3. Growing from isolated individual awareness into process group engagement is evolution in process.

Heart is calm

1. Emergencies are a state of mind. We don't do them anymore.

2. When leaders are centered, this communicates a state of well-being that all stakeholders feel and appreciate.

3. Panic is fear. Fear causes desperate behavior. We don't need to work this way. We've outgrown it.

Heart is open

1. We're always willing to consider challenges. Can we figure out an amazing new product? Let's try. Can we integrate people who don't speak English? Why not. They'll learn.

2. There is pain in throwing out thinking and habits that don't serve growth. But the excitement to grow heals this quickly.

3. Heart is courage to be present right now, to meet challenges with eyes open, knowing that together we can find a way.

Heart appreciates

1. What employees get from heart culture is continued adult development. Many workers aren't even aware this kind of growth is possible. They overflow with gratitude at how their lives improve.

2. Receiving heartfelt appreciation is a leader's highest reward. We hear it as a request to keep going.

3. The beauty is making heart culture available and seeing how people pick it up, how happy they become.

Heart expands and includes

1. As a company develops heart, a natural sense of inclusion results.
2. Working with heart confirms and satisfies a deep need for emotional connection.
3. Positive human connection in the workplace is heart culture.
4. People in the workplace long for meaning, let's give it to them.

Appendix

1. Language—Associate vs. Non-associate

Associate	Non-associate
Accountable/responsible	Entitled
Collaborate	Isolated
Conscientious	Indifferent
Customer-driven (internal and external)	Works for a paycheck
Dependable	Inconsistent
Desire	Required
Engaged	Disconnected
Works in a team	Works alone
Flexible	Resists change
Flow	Push or pull through
Initiative	Tell me what to do
Innovative	Complacent
Interdependent	Dependent
Learns from mistakes	Fears consequences of mistakes
Likes to learn	Teach me, train me, tell me
Makes decisions	Needs approval from others
Motivated	8:00 and hit the gate
Positive contributor	Going through motions
Risk taker	Afraid to make mistakes
Sharing	Territorial
Team success	Self-success
Trusting, trustworthy	Skeptical, untrustworthy
We	Me

2. Language—Lead vs. Manage

Lead	*Manage*
Engage	Direct
Influence	Control
Question/Listen	Tell/Do
Learn	Instruct
Motivate	Dominate
Integrate	Separate
Multiple Rights	I'm Right
Dialogue	Argue
Invite	Command
Ours	Mine

3. Further reading (Alpha by Title)

Action Inquiry: The secret of timely and transforming leadership, William R Torbert, Susanne R Cook-Greuter, Berrett-Koehler, 2004

Be Yourself, Everyone Else is Already Taken: Transform your life with the power of authenticity, Mike Robbins, Jossey-Bass, 2009

Beyond Reengineering: How the process-centered organization is changing our work and our lives, Michael Hammer, HarperBusiness, 1997

Conscious Capitalism: Liberating the heroic spirit of business, John Mackey and Rajendra Sisodia, Harvard Business Review Press, 2014

Create a World That Works: Tools for personal and global transformation, Alan Seale and Cheryl Dorsey, Weiser Books, 2011

Creating a Learning Culture: Strategy, technology, and practice, James G. Clawson and Marcia Conner, Cambridge University Press, 2004

The Fifth Discipline: The art and practice of the learning organization, Peter M. Senge, Doubleday, 2006

Firms of Endearment: How world-class companies profit from passion and purpose, Rajendra S. Sisodia and Jagdish N. Sheth, Pearson FT Press, second edition, 2014

The Generational Imperative: Understanding generational differences in the workplace, marketplace, and living room, Chuck Underwood, Generational Imperative, Incorporated, 2007

The Goal: A process of ongoing improvement, Eliyahu M. Goldratt and Jeff Cox, North River Press, 30th anniversary edition, 2012

How: Why how we do anything means everything, Dov Seidman, Wiley, 2011

A New Earth: Awakening to your life's purpose, Eckhart Tolle, Penguin, reprint edition, 2008

Presence: Human purpose and the field of the future, Peter M. Senge and C. Otto Scharmer, Crown Business, reprint edition, 2008

Switch: How to change things when change is hard, Chip Heath, Dan Heath, Crown Business, 2010

A Theory of Everything: An integral vision for business, politics, science and spirituality, Ken Wilber, Shambhala, 2001

Theory U: Leading from the future as it emerges, C. Otto Scharmer, Berrett-Koehler Publishers, 2009

The Tipping Point: How little things can make a big difference, Malcolm Gladwell, Back Bay Books, 2002

Transforming Your Leadership Culture, John B. McGuire, Gary Rhodes, Jossey-Bass, 2009

Type Talk at Work: How the 16 personality types determine your success on the job, Otto Kroeger, Janet M. Thuesen, Hile Rutledge, Delta, revised edition, 2002

The Values-Driven Organization: Unleashing human potential for performance and profit, Richard Barrett, Routledge, 2013

Winning with Accountability: The secret language of high-performing organizations, Henry J. Evans, CornerStone Leadership Institute, sixth edition, 2008

The 21 Indispensable Qualities of a Leader: Becoming the person others will want to follow, John C. Maxwell, Thomas Nelson, second edition, 2007

4. Glossary

Analects: Also known as, Analects of Confucius. Analects means "edited conversations" and is a collection of sayings and ideas written between 475 BC and 221 BC.

AQAL: "All Quadrants, All Levels" a multidimensional integral map of stages, lines, and levels of development; see Ken Wilber, A Brief History of Everything.

AT: Abrasive Technology, Inc.

CCL: Center for Creative Leadership

Holistic: Concept of the whole, in which all parts are interconnected. In medicine it is treatment of the whole person in contrast to treating isolated symptoms. In manufacturing it is an understanding of how all interconnected parts work together and the consequences of small and large changes.

Holon: A basic unit, and complete system in itself. Every holon is part of a larger system. For example, atoms are things in themselves. Molecules are a collection of atoms. A molecule has a distinct identity, yet it's also a thing in itself and it includes atoms. Molecules combine to form more complex structures, and so on.

Job jar: A repository of tasks and requests for help to be accessed by workers without a task. This can be an actual jar containing slips of paper on which are written requests, or, less literally, a person coordinating available resources and needs within a PCO environment.

Integral: Inclusive and comprehensive; the ability to see yourself and the world around you in more continuous, effective, and meaningful ways.

MBTI®: Myers-Briggs Type Indicator is an assessment tool designed to measure decision-making and communications preferences based on how people see themselves and the world.

Mindfulness: A state of awareness of what is present: bodily sensations, thoughts, and feelings; synonymous with presence.

Meditation: A quiet practice of focused concentration.

Process: A collection of sequential tasks. In a PCO environment processes are defined by function, such as finance, assembly, or customer service.

PCO: Process-centered organization, originated by Michael Hammer, replaces functional hierarchies, with flattened corporate structures based on processes (see above) and removal of cross-functional boundaries leading to more agile and effective operations.

SBI: Developed by CCL, Situation Impact Behavior is one of many communication feedback tools.

Servant leader: Describes a high state of psychological development; someone who is remover of obstacles, shares power, and helps others to achieve, in contrast to hoarding power and using it for control.

Spirituality: A subjective experience of transformation; including psychological growth, independent of religious ideals, or in accordance with them.

Transformative: Holistic growth toward higher states of being, meaning, satisfaction, and effectiveness.

Transactional: Linear thought and action; finding solutions to existing problems.

About the Authors

Tanya L. Patrella is co-founder and president of Manufacturing with Heart, Inc., a consulting and coaching company for small manufacturing businesses. She is an executive coach and human resources consultant. Tanya was an executive for Abrasive Technology, Inc., a worldwide manufacturer of superabrasive grinding wheels and tools. During her 25 years, she was vice president of administration, marketing, human resources and coach for the global leadership team.

As an original member of Abrasive's long-term business strategy team, Tanya has in-depth experience in organizational and leadership development, coaching leadership team members, as well as in global business and compliance, project management, and acquisition integrations.

She holds a BA in business administration from The Ohio State University and is certified in the Myers-Briggs Type Inventory and FIRO-B assessments for improving self-awareness.

In addition to her corporate successes, Tanya loves helping others through career coaching people in transition—young folks just starting out or anyone in transition in careers or wanting to be!

She also enjoys gardening, reading, learning, yoga, meditation, time with her three sisters and two daughters, a good Oregon Pinot Noir, fine dining, and walking in the woods.

Loyal M. (Butch) Peterman, Jr. co-founded Abrasive Technology, Inc., a leading manufacturer of superabrasive grinding wheels and tools with ten facilities around the world. In 1992, he became sole owner and President.

Butch co-founded Manufacturing with Heart, Inc. to share his leadership experience with small manufacturing businesses. He is an executive coach and business consultant.

As the leader of Abrasive's long-term Business Strategy Team, he created a profitable company with a positive and productive workplace based on unique organizational structure, early adopter of technologies, and culture centered on his core belief that "People Can be Trusted."

Butch holds BS and MS degrees in Mechanical Engineering from the University of Cincinnati, an MBA from Xavier University and is EQ certified. His career began as an engineer at General Electric Aviation and in market development at GE Superabrasives before opening his own company. He also holds several global patents.

He has received recognition as EY's Entrepreneur Of The Year in Manufacturing, is a founding board member of The Ohio Foundation for Entrepreneurial Education (OFEE), president and board member of the Industrial Diamond Association of America, and served as treasurer of The Country Club at Muirfield Village.

Butch enjoys connecting with people, engineering, making things simple, change, inventing, playing golf, the stock market, real estate investing, travel, fine dining, wines & champagnes, learning, yoga, and meditation.

Manufacturing
with
Heart

Exists to help others
Cultivate a Positive & Productive Workplace™

Where Employees:
- *Are Trusted*
- *Collaborative, Compassionate & Caring*
- *Innovative & Involved*
- *Love to Come to Work Every Day*

Through Systematic Integration of:
- *Employee & Leadership Vertical Development (Everyone Development)*
- *Process Centered Organizational Structure*
- *Policies / Guidelines to Create Trust*

Outcomes:
- *A Positive and Productive Workplace*
- *Improved productivity, quality and profitability*
- *Faster & better decision making*
- *Reduced employee turnover*

How:
We have strategies that have been tried, tested, implemented and they work!

www.manufacturingwithheart.com